A People's Guide To Tarot

A Primer For Everyone

Rhyd Wildermuth

A People's Guide To Tarot

A Primer For Everyone

Rhyd Wildermuth

First published 1 September, 2024
by RITONA Books
3, rue de Wormeldange
Rodenbourg, 6955
LUXEMBOURG

Design, Layout, and Editing by
RITONA Books

Cover Image includes CC-BY-SA work from
Freepik and Rawpixel

Find out more about our works at:
ABEAUTIFULRESISTANCE.COM

Within

How to Use This Guide

New to Tarot? Already experienced but want to learn more? Perfect, either way. This book is subtitled "a primer for everyone," because, well, that's who it's for: everyone.

Really often, or really *too often*, books on Tarot or related practices use a lot of difficult language and complicated ideas without ever really explaining what they actually mean. Occultists, especially, tend to do what academics do, which is try to sound really interesting by hiding what they're saying, or using words even they don't really understand. That's not to say they're actually not intelligent, but they're definitely not making things very clear for anyone.

Universities cost a lot of money, and so do expensive occult books, and spending so much money to learn things makes some people feel like they're part of an elite group. Or, maybe that's why they spend so much money — they want to feel elite.

This book isn't for elites, and neither is Tarot. In fact, Tarot has quite often been something very common and very working class. So, too, were the playing cards which were based on Tarot, which is why lots of upper-middle class Protestant-types in England and the United States made laws against playing with them.

In other words, Tarot belonged to the common people, which is why this book is called "A People's Guide to Tarot." And the word "primer" is a bit of a joke I'm playing on those stuffy Protestants from the 18th and 19th centuries. See, "primers" were often religious books written by ministers and similar sorts, and they were full of instructions on how to be a polite and diligent worker or a polite and obedient housewife. And many of those primers also told you to avoid playing with cards, and dancing, and anything else that might be truly fun.

This primer won't tell you to do those things. Also, it's for you, regardless of where you come from and how much you already know.

You'll see that the book is divided into two parts. The first part explains what the Tarot is, how it works, and how to do readings. It also gives you some tips on understanding the relationships between the cards.

The second half contains interpretations of each of the cards, based on my own experience. I don't claim my interpretations are the "correct" ones, because that's anyway not how Tarot works. But, I do give some interpretations that might be a bit different from other guides, and when this happens, I tell you both the "traditional" interpretations and also mine.

Now, you can use this book any way you'd like. It's for you, after all. And there are at least two good ways to go about reading it. First, you can read through the entire book, and then try out a few readings using the interpretations in this guide. That's definitely one way, and probably a good one. Or, you can just start using the interpretations immediately, and then read the chapters in the first section later. That's also a really good way.

And you can, of course, mix these two approaches. That's actually what I did when I first started reading Tarot, and it worked pretty well for me. So maybe read as much as you'd like in the first part, try out a few readings, and then read more when you'd like.

Honestly, though, whatever you do with this book is fine.

Also, you'll need a Tarot, if you don't have one already. There are many, many, many good ones out there, and a few really strange ones. If you've never had a Tarot, starting with the most classic one — "the Rider-Waite" or "Rider-Waite-Colman" — might be a good idea. Most modern decks are based on this one, with a few modifications, so you'll do fine with any of those, as well. Just be aware that some Tarot versions change the names and even the ordering of the cards, or add extra cards not in traditional decks, and so this might get confusing if you're new to Tarot.

I hope you find this book really helpful. I really enjoyed writing it for you.

—Rhyd Wildermuth

Part One: About Tarot

Tarot and Divination

When you dream, you see images and interact with people even though you are asleep. Some of those images are familiar, and some of those people are just like the humans you know in your waking life. Other times, people you've never met seem to show up and tell you things, or you visit places and see things that you're not even sure really exist in the world.

Sometimes, what happens in your dreams makes sense and seems to relate to your everyday life. Other times, it's all so strange and unfamiliar that you wake up confused and can barely recall what happened.

The part of you that dreams is sometimes called the unconscious, and there are complex theories about why your dreaming-self encounters all these symbols. But an older way of looking at dreaming was that some part of you — maybe your soul, or your spirit, or whatever — traveled to a place it could only easily reach during a dream. And in that place, you met with other souls who were also dreaming, or with the dead, or with spirits, and especially with beings or personalities that actually lived in that place.

One name for that place is "the imaginal," or the *mundus imaginalis* ("the imaginal world"). And obviously, the imaginal is related to our word "imagine," so I need to clear up something immediately:

The imaginal isn't an imaginary place.

Instead, it's a kind of faculty or sense we humans have, somewhere between reason and the unconscious. Imagination is one way that we use this faculty, but it's not the only way. It's a bit like how doing math in your head is a kind of thinking, but it's not the only kind of thinking we do.

There's an easier way to understand this. Consider the difference between intelligence and intuition, and how we think of them as coming from two different parts of our bodies. We think of intelligence as something that happens in our minds. But then we think of intuition as something that happens in the rest of our body. We say that we have "a gut feeling" that something isn't right, or that someone gives us goosebumps, or that a situation "feels wrong." In other words, we already believe there are different ways of getting knowledge, and we locate these ways in different places of our bodies.

The imaginal is like this. The knowledge we get from it is in the form of images that seem to have a life of their own.

In dreams, those images move about and tell us things. In Tarot and other forms of divination, those images are usually not moving about, and what they have to tell us is in a language we don't always understand.

The imaginal isn't in the mind. Where it actually is, I don't know. The older ways of understanding it used a completely different system for describing knowledge from our Western scientific model. In their system, they thought of different kinds of knowledge (bodily, mental, unconscious, imaginal, divine) as different spheres around a human. But most people don't think of knowledge this way anymore, and now we don't have a good way to describe the imaginal.

But if it helps, you can think of the imaginal as the knowledge sense of the soul (if you believe in such a thing) or the unconscious. And this knowledge sense is able to perceive some things that other senses (like touch) cannot.

That doesn't mean it's a "higher" or "better" kind of sense. Touch tells you things that taste cannot, while taste can give you information that touch never can. The senses are all different, with each one being really good for some kinds of knowledge and not good for others.

And here's one more complication. We modern people consider our brain to be the center of our mind and all of our thinking, like it's the master of the body rather than just some part of it. But the brain isn't a sense organ. Instead, its role is to interpret all the senses coming in to it, to decide what they mean, and then to make decisions based on those interpretations.

Usually, the brain gets things right. Sometimes, it gets things very, very wrong. For instance, anxiety is often the brain interpreting sensations incorrectly. Maybe you're tired or hungry or thirsty, but the brain misses what is actually happening and then decides that everyone hates you or that something really bad is going to happen.

So, if the role of the brain is to interpret information from your senses, and the imaginal is a sense, then you can understand how things might not always get interpreted correctly. When you read Tarot, your imaginal sense gets information that your brain then tries to interpret. And the point of this book is to help you do that better

Now, I'm hardly the only person to write a guide to Tarot. In fact, there are thousands of guidebooks to Tarot, and many of them are really useful. In my experience, the best ones are those that don't try to do all the interpretations for you, but instead give you clues and hints that will help you learn to read for yourself. And so, that's what I'll try to do for you, too.

Now, I mentioned that Tarot is a kind of divination, but I didn't explain what divination actually is. The root of the word — divine — gives you a really good clue here, and the original Latin from which we get the word meant "to be inspired by a god."

Maybe — like me — you believe in many gods. Or, maybe you believe in one god or no gods at all. Regardless of how you see this, it's helpful to understand what Roman pagans thought was happening when someone was "inspired." That word literally meant "to breathe in," and so it was like a person had just breathed in a bit of a god.

In other words, it wasn't necessarily that a god was telling you something. Instead, you'd caught a whiff of a god, a bit like catching the scent of blossoms on a spring day, or the smell of the first drops of rain, or an exotic perfume. In that breath, you understood something you didn't understand before. Or you had an idea, or a surge of creativity, and because of this you were able to then do something quite amazing.

That's how I think you should look at divination. It's a moment where you try to get inspiration, to breathe in something powerful and helpful, and when it works you can then see things in a better way. Where you decide that inspiration actually comes from isn't up to me, and it's anyway a lot less relevant than what you do with that inspiration.

What's quite amazing about Tarot as a form of divination is that it's useful no matter the spiritual framework you are using. That's because our imaginal sense doesn't make the same kinds of distinctions about spiritual or metaphysical matters as our minds do. Again, think of the more physical senses, like hearing. Your eardrums take in information about the world all the time, vibrating in response to the invisible waves of energy that we call sound. But your ears don't interpret that information, and they can't just close out some sounds because they don't believe in them.

The imaginal is like that, too. When you read Tarot, you'll get a lot of information from the imaginal. But it doesn't actually tell you what those things mean, nor where they come from. Maybe it's some part of you that is speaking, or some buried memory, or a dead ancestor, or a god, or something else entirely. But the information you get, and how you interpret it, is what's most important.

What is Tarot?

Tarot's specific origins are unclear and quite contested. People have some pretty big online fights about this matter, and I really suggest not getting involved in those. And anyway, the internet is never a very nice place.

The Tarot that most of us use now is a composite form of divination, meaning that it combines symbols from several older forms of cartomancy. Cartomancy means "divination by cards." The second half of the word derives from a Greek word that referred to prophets, oracles, and the spirits they worked with.

Cartomancy has been practiced by several different cultures, but the earliest evidence of Tarot is from the 15th century in what is now Italy. Some think that Tarot was originally just a card game that later came to be used for divination. It's also likely (maybe even more so) that its usage as a game was a way of hiding its divinatory aspects from Church authorities. Also, most forms of divination usually have a more common activity associated with it. For example, coins are money, but a coin toss uses that money for a very simple divination.

The Tarot most people are familiar with, the Rider-Waite (or the Rider-Waite-Smith) Tarot, is quite new. It was created by Arthur E. Waite and painted by Pamela Colman Smith, both of whom were members of an esoteric magical society in England called The Golden Dawn. The Rider part of the name comes from its first publisher, William Rider & Son, and it was first published in 1909.

Many of the images that Pamela Colman Smith painted are based loosely on older Tarots, while others were conceived through the work of Arthur E. Waite and his interpretations of another occultist, Éliphas Lévi. Arthur E. Waite was a historian of Western occult practices, and he was not only a member of the Golden Dawn but also of the Freemasons. So, many of its symbols and images borrow heavily from these traditions, as well as from Western astrology and Islamic alchemist traditions, while some are completely new.

People definitely read Tarot before this version was born. Before 1909, many readers used the very popular Tarot of Marseilles, though there were quite a few others in circulation as well. And some even used mundane playing cards, which are anyway derived from those original Tarots.

Most newer Tarot decks borrow heavily from the Rider-Waite deck. And there are some that do not at all borrow from Rider-Waite, usually called "oracle cards." These can be quite useful, of course, but if you're just starting to learn, this guide will be most helpful if your deck is more traditional.

And if you're wondering, no: no Tarot deck is more "true" than any other. In fact, the first step to learning any divination is to let go of our really strange modern idea there can be only one true thing. We get taught that truth is always a one-to-one correspondence, that something must always mean one thing and not also another one.

To see the problem with this idea, consider the "truth" of poetry. What does a poem "really mean?" If it's really good poetry, then it cannot be reduced to any one singular meaning. Or what does a painting mean, or a song, or any other work of art?

It's the same with Tarot. No card has a singular meaning. Instead, they have lots of meanings, and to interpret them we have to understand their relationships to each other, and also to ourselves and our situation. As with a poem, subtle meanings build upon each other, shading or tinting each subsequent image. Think of the way color shifts and fades into other colors in a painting, or the way harmonies play in a symphony, or how sunlight illuminates a landscape differently in each hour, and you're closer to understanding the "truth" of how Tarot works.

The skill of interpreting these relationships cannot really be taught, but it can be learned and developed. Eastern spiritual traditions such as Taoism are founded upon this kind of thinking-feeling, so reading the *Tao Te Ching* may be very helpful. But just as helpful would be sitting in a garden all day, or walking in a forest, letting light and sound and other sensations wash over you.

Reading Tarot

Even though you can read books about Tarot like this one, you cannot read Tarot like a book. Instead, it's a lot more like reading a poem or like reading a person. You have to approach it with a playful curiosity, an openness to the world more common in children than in adults.

Of course, you're probably going to read Tarot to try to find out something, and you're going to be bringing a lot of emotions into the reading. Maybe you're worried about the future, or about a relationship situation. Maybe you're in a moment of confusion, or of sadness, or of great excitement. And no matter how hard you try, all these emotions are going to color the way you interpret the cards.

That's okay. Our emotions also inform how we interpret art. We'll experience a song that makes us feel really good, or that seems to speak to exactly the sadness we're feeling at the moment, in a profoundly different way than we would if there were no emotions involved. So, there's no need to try to suppress what you're feeling. Instead, it's much better to acknowledge those feelings and see what they want to teach you. In fact, there's an entire suit of cards, the cups, that's about learning how to do this.

Also, you're probably going to use Tarot to try to understand situations, relationships, and others around you. That's fine, too. More than fine, actually, because the Tarot is particularly good at teaching us how to understand those things.

And Tarot is particularly useful as a method of self-development. Reading Tarot helps you learn how the processes of your own mind, your memories, your surroundings, and those around you shape the way you see the world, yourself, and others. This kind of self-development is an essential skill for other spiritual frameworks, too. If you don't know how your mind works, if you don't understand your own tendencies, biases, or fears, and especially if you don't know how to listen to your own instincts and intuition, then you'll have a difficult time telling the difference between spiritual experiences and wishful thinking.

When you use Tarot this way, think of the cards like the mirrored surface of a still lake. Your thoughts will reflect back to you, as will your hopes, fears, biases, and everything else. Some of that stuff will appear to be at the bottom of the lake, some of it will be behind you in the sky, some of it will be on your own face. And sometimes, something else will be in your vision that you couldn't see when you tried to look directly.

Now, many people develop all kinds of interesting rituals and beliefs around the cards themselves. Some people think that the cards are spirits, or that to be a good Tarot reader you need to summon a spirit to live in them. Others develop interesting taboos around them — for instance, keeping them stored in a black cloth bag to prevent them from picking up negative energies, or cleansing them under a new moon if someone else touched them. Some claim that only certain people can truly read Tarot, and they come up with interesting ideas about psychic powers. And during the readings, they use interesting things like crystals and incense and candles, or they say certain interesting prayers, and they especially focus on interesting ways to shuffle and pull the cards.

All these ideas and rituals and props are definitely ... interesting. And that's all I should really say about them, because I'm trying to be polite. But you won't see any of these things in this guide.

Whenever we learn or start a new practice, magical or otherwise, we often over-complicate everything. People just beginning a gym or fitness program, for example, tend to spend a lot of money on branded athletic clothing and shoes, on supplements, on over-priced water bottles, and all kinds of other things they don't actually need. The same goes for those starting a garden for the first time — we purchase too many seeds and plant starts, as well as more tools than we could possibly use. And while all that enthusiasm is a really important part in starting any practice (that's what the aces are about!), we can make things so complicated for ourselves that we soon give up.

When many people start reading Tarot, they do the same thing. I certainly did, making everything far more complicated than it needed to be. But I'm going to try to help you avoid that mistake.

What you actually need to read Tarot is the Tarot itself. That's it. No spells, no prayers, no special incense or candles or anything else. You don't even need this book. Other things (including this book) can certainly help, while other things can get in the way. Don't stress too much about any of this, and try not to overcomplicate this stuff.

Shuffling

As I just mentioned, it's easy to overcomplicate things. Try not to do that. Instead, just shuffle the Tarot deck seven times. It's also okay to shuffle more (some shuffle nine times, which is closer to mathematical "randomization"). But if you want the cards to be mostly not in the same order as the last time, don't shuffle fewer than seven times.

Again, there are some interesting ideas about energy entering the cards when you shuffle, or how it's important to focus on your question while you shuffle. I find none of this actually matters, but you're absolutely welcome to try.

The Question

When I read Tarot for myself, I sometimes ask a question after I've shuffled and before I've drawn the cards. I don't always ask a question, though, and you don't always need to, either.

Asking a question does have an important purpose, and doing so can be quite powerful by itself. Consider how we very rarely ask ourselves things. When's the last time you've asked yourself if you're happy, or satisfied, or if you're doing your best, or if you're lacking anything? We almost never ask such things, except when there's a crisis. In Tarot, you get to learn to ask these questions before a crisis, and we can get a clearer idea of the results of certain actions or decisions that we usually don't consider otherwise.

In other words, we rarely reflect on our life, but with Tarot or other methods of divination, we make the decision to do so. You may not always understand what you see or even like it, because you might find there are many unexamined things about yourself or your situation that surprise you. It's also equally likely that you'll discover some unnoticed joy or wonder, something you didn't see because you'd never stopped to think about it before.

It's best to phrase the question simply, and to realize that often what we think are questions are really just statements. For instance, consider the question, "is my wife going to leave me?" You've not actually asked a question at all, but rather made the statement: "I'm worried my wife is going to leave me." In such cases, the question can instead be rephrased more helpfully along the lines of, "I'm afraid my wife is going to leave me, why do I feel this way?"

In other words, it's best to ask a question that relates back to yourself in some way. If you focus too much on external situations or how others are feeling or doing, you'll often get confusing results. You also have no control over other people (you *do* know this … right?), and so none of the information you'll get will be helpful.

Anyway, in situations like that, what you truly need to know is something quite different, and very often the cards will reveal this. Let's say you had an argument with someone you love and now you're not talking to each other. You might be tempted to then ask the cards why that person was so stubborn and what you can do to convince them you were right. But then, the cards that appear might then direct you back to your own role in that argument, and even point out that you're letting your own opinions or perspectives get in the way of your friendship (yes — there are cards for that, like the Five of Swords and the Five of Wands).

Sometimes, it doesn't even matter what question you ask. Occasionally, I've had experiences where I've asked a specific question but then gotten the answer to a completely different one, instead. When that first happened, I was tempted to reshuffle the cards and draw again, but quickly realized that something (the imaginal, or the Tarot, or something else altogether) was actually ignoring my question because there was something more important I needed to know.

All this is to say that you also shouldn't worry too much about getting the questions "right." This takes practice, and even really experienced Tarot readers can find their reading hijacked by a question they didn't think to ask. You'll figure this out as you go along.

And as I said earlier, you don't even need to ask a question at all. For a full year, I tried a practice recommended by John Michael Greer in which you perform a divination every day. These were essentially the equivalent of "weather reports," like looking outside the window to see if it was sunny or rainy or if you need a coat. And I learned much more about reading Tarot from that practice than I did when I tried to get the questions perfect.

Drawing the Cards

Most guidebooks recommend what's called the "Celtic Cross" spread. In that common form of reading, you lay out ten cards, with six of them forming a circle or a wheel, and the last four placed in a vertical line to the right side of the wheel.

This kind of reading can be useful, certainly, as can any other layout of the cards. Yet the longer I read Tarot, the more I felt that this layout was really overcomplicating things. Now, after more than twenty-five years of reading Tarot for myself and others, the three card spread is the only one I use, and it's also the only one I recommend to others.

One of the reasons why people use more complicated spreads is because they believe that the more cards you use, the more information you'll get about a question. On the surface, this is certainly true, but more information doesn't actually translate into more insight. Our modern lives are so full of information that it can often be really difficult to decide what's actually relevant, what's important, and what's just noise. The same problem can apply to complicated spreads.

Again, there's nothing wrong with other card layout schemes, and none of them are superior to the others. And if you're just starting out and really feel like you want to use the others, that's great. The interpretations and suggestions in this guide will be useful for any kind of spread you choose. But if you start feeling overwhelmed with these methods, it's not you — it's the spread. Instead of giving up or deciding Tarot is too difficult, try the three card spread.

There are two ways to lay out the cards in a three card spread — horizontally and vertically. They're both essentially the same, except that the visual relationship of the cards to each other shifts slightly.

Here's the horizontal version:

I also recommend sometimes re-arranging the cards in a vertical line, with the "past" card at the bottom and the "future" card at the top, and instead thinking of them as parts of a tree:

Now, these two arrangements are not actually different spreads, but rather just two ways of looking at the same cards. Keeping both of them in mind — and even sometimes re-arranging the positions during a reading — helps you remember that linear time is only one way of looking at things. In fact, until very recently, the idea of time as a straight line was practically unheard of in human societies.

In other words, what we think of as "past" isn't always accurate. We might imagine something that happened before the present time no longer exists, but the past doesn't actually work that way. Instead, the past is a lot like the roots of a tree. Because we don't see those roots, it's easy for us to forget they exist. But without those roots, there would be no tree.

The same goes for our understanding of the future. We often imagine that the future is a destination we're heading to, as if the point of our lives is to "arrive" somewhere else. Because of this, we then imagine that the future already exists — like the end of a book we're reading — and this can lead us to feel powerless in our current circumstances, or to expect results without any real effort to manifest them. Instead, it's often helpful to think of the future as the branches and leaves of a tree, the manifestation of growth fed by the roots (the past) and sustained by the trunk (the present). And just like leaves absorb sunlight for the rest of the tree, the future also feeds our present and our past.

Now, to be clear, you don't need to fully understand these other ways of looking at time to read Tarot. In fact, reading Tarot is one of the ways that this kind of understanding develops. The more you engage with the cards, the more your mind will start to grasp these additional relationships, and it will eventually become quite automatic for you.

Past

Passing influences
Foundations
Roots of an issue

Present

Current influences
The core of an issue
Your state of mind
Current challenge

Future

Upcoming influences
Possible results or
consequences
The path forward

The Roles of Cards in the Past Position

When a card arrives in the first position of a spread, whether you are reading horizontally or vertically, it is giving you information about an important root or foundation of the current situation. And just like the foundation of a house or the roots of a tree are often invisible to us, this information may not have been something you have noticed before.

One way of looking at cards that arrive here is to think of them as previous choices or a specific influence that created your present circumstances. Of course, many choices and many influences may have been at play, but the card that appears here is the one that is most relevant to what is signified by the second card.

Sometimes, this card can instead be trying to draw your attention to the way you look at the past, rather than the actual past itself. Sometimes, we misunderstand previous events, or we interpreted them in an unhelpful way. This is especially common with difficult childhood memories or traumatic relationship events like break-ups. At the time they occurred, we may not have had the capability to really understand what was happening, or our emotional states might have led us to come to false conclusions. For example, being bullied as a child might have led us to internalize the cruel things that were said to us. As adults, we are in better positions to re-interpret those situations and let go of the unhealthy beliefs we adopted in response to those events.

Because of this, the cards that appear here can sometimes be quite uncomfortable at first glance. There might even be times when you feel the card is scolding you in some way, especially if it appears to be pointing out some way in which you're responsible for an unpleasant current situation. If this happens, it's especially important to be curious about your emotional reactions in a kind and neutral way. There's important information in your feelings that will help you understand the situation better.

Another role of the card in the past position is to give you insight into a recent influence or state of mind that is just passing out of your life, or a previous problem that has now been resolved. These can often be accomplishments that you haven't yet acknowledged, previous struggles you've successfully overcome, or certain waves of activity or emotions that helped get you to this point but are no longer factors. Especially when court cards appear in this position, they can be referring to the completion of certain cycles or life stages.

The Role of Cards in the Present Position

In my own readings, I often find the cards that arrive in the present position to be the most informative. They can also be the most surprising and — at the very same time — the most obvious. In fact, sometimes these cards feel like a little prank from the Tarot, like it's telling me something cosmically obvious and I'm apparently the only one who didn't notice it yet.

That's because the role of the card in this position is to tell you about your current situation the way a close friend might. People who know us very well can often say things to us in a way that we are most likely to understand, to give us helpful criticism without coming across as judgmental, or to give us profound insights into our emotional states that we cannot give ourselves.

We tend to turn to such friends on certain matters, because we trust that they will not alter their words out of fear of offending us. When discussing issues we are facing, they'll often notice times when we are deluding ourselves, or getting ourselves into the same kinds of problems over and over again, and they're better able than others to give us advice we really need to hear. And sometimes, they can say exactly the right thing to help us see ourselves better, confirming the very best parts of us, while helping us to overcome the rougher parts.

It's quite helpful when interpreting the present position to imagine such a friend speaking to us. The card that appears there is trying to point out the obvious in a way that we'll understand, or to give us helpful feedback about a situation that we might have missed.

The role of cards in this position is also to help identify current influences on your life and current mental or emotional states. Sometimes, it can be a confirmation that your current choices are the correct ones, and sometimes quite the opposite. However, if it seems to be warning you or telling you that a current situation is not as you thought it was, you probably already knew this already.

Remember that this second position is not just the present but also like the trunk of a tree. The card in the first position and the card in this position are connected in some way, and much of the lifelong work of Tarot is learning how to notice those connections.

The Role of Cards in the Future Position

The best response I can give when someone asks me if it's possible to tell the future with Tarot is to smile and say, *"depends on what you want to tell it."* That's because, as I mentioned earlier, our Western idea of linear time is not really accurate. The past isn't dead, and the future isn't a final destination.

Just as the branches and leaves are outgrowths of the roots and trunk of a tree, the cards that appear in this position are telling you what will grow from the relationship between the two previous cards. You can think of this as a potential or likely "result" or "manifestation."

By seeing it this way, you are able to gain really useful insight into your current situation or the question at hand. For instance, the card might give you a confirmation that the choices you are making now will lead to the outcomes you intend; or, you could get some important information that leads you to change what you're doing.

As with other positions, you might often find that some part of you already knew what the card is telling you. For instance, if you've just entered a really passionate relationship that has some destructive elements, the card in this position might warn you about the result of ignoring those red flags. This information probably won't surprise you, but you might also struggle with acknowledging the reality of the situation. And in such a scenario, you still need to make decisions about what to do with that information.

Another role of the cards in this position is to give you insight into upcoming influences in your life. Here, the information is a lot like a weather forecast. Meteorologists make their forecasts by collecting data on high and low pressure systems and comparing that data to what typically happens in such scenarios. Though they cannot ever predict the weather with 100% accuracy, they can accurately predict that the conditions which result in certain kinds of weather events will arrive.

That's also how to understand cards in this position. You can accurately predict what conditions or influences are arriving and then prepare for them, just like you might prepare for rainy conditions by taking an umbrella when you leave the house.

And sometimes, cards in this position can play a helpful little trick on you. For instance, if you're feeling depressed, and a card in this position seems to tell you that everything's about to get better, guess what? You'll feel better, maybe even immediately. Did the card predict this, or did it make that happen? Either way, remember: the future isn't a destination, and sometimes you try to tell the future, and sometimes the future tells you.

The Relationship of the Cards

In a three card spread, using only upright cards, there are 456,456 possible combinations. If someone were to write a guidebook with just two sentences explaining the meaning of each combination, the result would be a book with over 34,000 pages.

And, even if such a book existed, it probably wouldn't be very useful. That's because the combinations of cards that appear in a reading can only be truly understood in the context of the person the reading is done for, and each card has multiple shades of meaning. It would be impossible to account for all of these possibilities in a guidebook, no matter its length.

If this sounds overwhelming, it's only because we've become over-reliant on a certain way of seeing the world and a specific way of gathering knowledge. We also rely heavily on just one sense — our sight — and forget that our other senses have things to tell us.

Tarot relies on an inherent human skill that oral societies know very well but that our literate societies forget even exists. That doesn't mean it's completely disappeared, though. When you listen to a poet or a skilled storyteller, this skill reawakens in you. And the more you read Tarot, the more powerful this skill becomes.

What exactly is this skill? I've heard it called many names, and none of them really fit. In fact, attempting to pin it down with a label is exactly the wrong way of understanding it. Categories and definitions are tools of written societies, not of oral ones.

So, when you lay out cards in your reading, try to think of them not as codes to be translated, but rather as parts of a story being told. And then, try to connect to other ways of knowing the world besides sight.

One way of doing this is to imagine the cards as chord changes in a song. Or, imagine being outside on a warm day, feeling sunlight on your skin while at the same time sensing the coolness of grass under your bare feet and a light breeze pass over you. Taste can also help here: imagine the cards as the subtle mix of textures and spices of a fragrant meal. Or, the way the air smells on a summer evening in a city just as it starts to rain, and how all those indescribable scents mix together to create an intoxicating perfume.

That's how the cards relate to each other, and you already have the skill to understand these relationships. You do this all the time with your other senses, and only need to learn to let yourself do this with Tarot, too.

The absolute best way to learn to understand the relationships of the cards is practice. The more you read Tarot, the more it will make sense to you, and the more confident you'll be in understanding the relationships between the cards.

It can also help to have someone more experienced do a reading for you, but even more effective is to ask someone to let you watch as they do a reading for themself, or to read examples of such readings. So, I'll include a few readings I've done for myself while writing this book, and explain how I came to the conclusions I did about the cards.

Reading One – A General Reading

I did this reading while writing the previous section of this book, and I didn't have a specific question in mind. Instead, I pulled the cards to get a general "weather report," to check in with myself and my current conditions.

Here's what I pulled:

The very first thing I noticed is that all three cards were Pentacles. That's a really clear indication that the reading relates to my physical life and material conditions.

Now, let me tell you a bit about my life at the moment. For the last eight months, I've been focused very heavily on weight lifting. I'm at the gym at least four days a week now, and have been strictly tracking the food I eat and restricting my calories.

This is new to me, though. I'm 47 years old, and only even started giving attention to my health just before I turned 40. Also, the amount of self-discipline this training has required has often felt overwhelming. I'm tired quite often, and some days it has been quite hard to feel like it's even worth all this effort.

At the same time, I've found that this physical training has also changed the way I look at the work I do. Being a writer and a book publisher means sitting still for many hours in front of a screen, which is pretty much the opposite of what I do at the gym. It's not been very easy to reach a balance between these two aspects of my life, and I've occasionally worried that I'll need to sacrifice one for the other.

So, with that context, you can maybe see why I laughed a bit when I pulled those three cards.

First of all, the *Two of Pentacles* in the past position appeared as a direct reference both to my fears about balancing these physical aspects of my life and also to the need to expand my physical existence. When I started this training, I wasn't sure I'd be able to keep at it because of the extra time commitment and discipline required, but I also really wanted to see what more I was capable of.

The present position, the *Eight of Pentacles*, is a very, very accurate description of my current state. In fact, I've thought about this card repeatedly in the previous months, especially whenever I've questioned whether or not this training has been worth it. Also, a few times I've needed to remind myself not to focus so much on the intended results. That's because I sometimes feel depressed when I think of how much more work there is to do, like it all feels so far away.

The *Knight of Pentacles* in the future position, then, appears both as a kind of promise that this self-discipline and hard work will be worth it, and also a reminder of the kind of existence this will lead to. By remaining committed to this, especially when it's really, really difficult, I'll develop the kind of patient and practical mindset this card describes. Also, I'll learn even more of what it needed to maintain the balance I've worried about.

Simultaneously, these three cards are also just as relevant to my work life, as well. I'm currently in the midst of an expansion project and will be soon taking on a much larger publishing role. This has meant a lot of extra work towards goals that aren't fully clear to me yet, and I've had to focus much more on the work in front of me rather than longer term planning. As with the gym training, these cards remind me that I'm approaching this situation in the best possible way at the moment.

Reading Two – A Relationship Reading

For this reading, which I drew just now as I started this section, I was curious for insight into my relationship with my husband.

First, I'll give you some background. About five months ago, my husband suffered from a debilitating psychological crisis brought on by a work burnout. Before that breakdown, he had been in an incredibly stressful and very unhealthy professional position that was doing real damage to his physical health and his sense of self, and it was also putting some very worrying strains on our relationship.

The breakdown was a difficult time for him, and it's taken him quite some time to begin the process of healing. Fortunately, he is being paid for the time off he needs, so there have been no financial fears.

Of course, it's also been a difficult time for me, especially because I needed to devote a lot of my time to helping him through the crisis. It's also required major adjustments of my work days and the way I use my free time. But it's also been a very positive thing, since the causes of our previous relationship strains are now gone.

Now, here are the cards which just appeared:

As I've mentioned many times, the cards that tend to appear are often quite unsurprising, and this is especially true for that first card, *The Tower*. When The Tower appears, it very often refers to external crises that needed to happen in order to change a situation. That's exactly how both I and my husband describe the mental breakdown he experienced. Without it, his health might have gotten even worse, and there were a few times it wasn't certain our relationship could survive the stress his job brought us both.

While the first card wasn't surprising, the second card wasn't immediately something that I had expected. The *Three of Cups* speaks to friendship, celebration, and the way our desires and emotional awareness expands through interactions with others. After a few moments of consideration, I then understood that it likely referred to the way that my husband and I are better able to communicate with each other and get to know each other better now that we have much more time together. This has certainly been one of the benefits of the crisis The Tower speaks to. But also, I've found that I've lately come to value even more certain friendships with people who were there for me during his crisis.

The third card, *The World*, gives me more information to interpret the second card, since both cards have meanings that include the idea of celebration. Also, when The World appears in the final position like this, it very often indicates the completion or fulfillment of a cycle or situation described in the previous cards. It's an incredibly positive card here, indicating that the crisis of The Tower (my husband's work burnout) will result in a much better situation for both of us. The Three of Cups between them also suggests that this transformation will be related to an expanded social life and a sense of joy and celebration, rather than the constant struggle and social isolation which preceded the crisis.

Reading Three: Self-Analysis

For this reading, I want to gain more insight into my feelings regarding a difficult problem I've not really been able to sort out.

Here's what happened. I took a commission for a large book project several years ago, and wrote it to what I felt was the best of my ability. The publisher was originally quite enthusiastic about the manuscript, and I was told it would be their leading book for that publishing season.

But then, just before publication, strange things happened, and there was quite a lot of internal and external pressure on the publisher not to promote my book. Also, the publicist stopped replying to my emails soon after it was published, and though the public reading events I did for the book were very well attended, the publisher didn't provide any real support for them and even didn't provide enough books for attendees who wanted to buy them.

I was never able to get clear answers as to what happened, and I've really struggled over the feeling that all the time and effort I put into writing that book was a complete waste. My experience with this even led to many moments where I wondered if I should just stop writing altogether.

So, that's the situation I'm curious about, and this is the first time I'll be pulling cards about it. Let's see what I can learn:

The first thing I did was to re-arrange the cards vertically, to remind myself that the past position is the foundation. That means that the idea of arriving at an emotionally-fulfilled state is at the root of my feelings around this issue, and I certainly don't feel that way about the situation. In fact, it's more accurate to say that what I was hoping for turned out not to be the end result at all. Tens are completions that lead to the understanding of what more is possible, and in a past or root position like this, they can sometimes also mean pre-occupation with an earlier goal.

So, the *Ten of Cups* seems to be telling me that my feelings about this situation are still influenced by what I thought the result would be. And I'll admit, I had some really high hopes, and I readily believed the initial statements from the publisher about its likely success and their willingness to promote it. But also, I really enjoyed writing the book, and it felt quite fulfilling. The Ten of Cups also seems like a kind reminder not to diminish the joy that came from completing such a large creative project, regardless of its results.

The *Six of Wands* is about recognition and success, and it seems like the exact opposite card I would have expected in the present or trunk position. That's because the book doesn't seem to have succeeded, and the complete failure of its publisher to promote it still feels like a refusal to recognize the work I did for it. But this may be why the card seems to have appeared: it's drawing my attention to the core issue, the reason why I feel so frustrated and sometimes depressed about the situation.

It's also possible that the Six of Wands means something else. I still get quite a few emails and messages from people who've read the book and found it incredibly helpful. In other words, it does actually get recognition, and it's possible I've overly focused on certain measures of success and missed more concrete ones. As I've said, the cards that appear in the present position are often like a close friend pointing out something you haven't noticed.

The third card, *Temperance*, is often about transformation and about finding creative paths to change a situation. My first thought with this card is that it's suggesting that it's soon the moment to work through these emotions and find a new way of understanding the situation. But Temperance can also sometimes refer to the process of a sword becoming tempered, and patience is an aspect of this process.

So, the three cards together seem to be suggesting a need to understand the situation in a different way, to let go of a previous preoccupation with what I thought success should look like, and to try to transform my emotions about the situation in a patient way. Or, they can all just be telling me to be patient.

Some readings are like this, by the way. You won't always get the answer you are hoping for, and you won't always even be certain you understood the meaning. In such cases, I highly recommend what I will do, which is to leave the question for a while and then come back to it again at another time.

Try not to obsess over the issue too much when this happens. Also, I really recommend not doing another reading just after one that doesn't give you the clear results you hoped for. If you do, you might find those subsequent readings to be even more confusing than the first. Take at least a day off before your next attempt.

The Internal Logic of Tarot

Learning to read Tarot is a lot like learning a new language. When we first start learning a language, we often try to translate the words into the one we normally speak. This works okay in the beginning, but eventually we also have to learn how the words relate to each other in their own language.

Part of that process is learning the internal logic or grammar of the new language, and sometimes this logic is completely different from what we're used to. For instance, many languages like English, French, and German usually put subjects before verbs, and then put objects after, in this way: *I throw the ball*. However, many other languages, like Japanese or Korean, put the object between the subject and verb, like: *I the ball throw.*

Fortunately, the internal logic or grammar of Tarot isn't as complicated as trying to learn a foreign language. However, if it were a language, it would be a lot more like written Chinese than like written English. That's because Chinese doesn't use an alphabet, but rather combines a series of strokes — which are really simplified drawings — together to form a word.

Tarot and Chinese writing have something else in common, too. The oldest Chinese writing is called "oracle bone script," because it was first used to record the results of divinations. This is also a bit like runes in Old Nordic languages. Runes were both the letters used to form words, and also a tool for divination.

The Major and Minor Arcana

Now, as I said, Tarot has an internal logic to it, and understanding this logic helps you understand the relationships between the cards. We'll start with the first part of this logic or grammar, which is the Major Arcana and the Minor Arcana.

The Major Arcana consists of 22 cards. These start with The Fool (0) and end with The World (21). They're called "Major" because the information or secrets they represent are more related to spiritual states of being, rather than everyday ways of being.

That doesn't mean they are therefore better or more important, and it's best not to treat them that way when they show up in a reading. A more helpful way of looking at them is that they are more like major themes or plot points in life, rather than the details or individual scenes which make up that life.

The Minor Arcana consists of 56 cards, and these are divided into suits (cups, swords, pentacles, and wands). Each of these suits is associated with an aspect of human existence (emotions, intellect, body, and will) corresponding to one of the elements (water, air, earth, and fire). And then, there's a further division in the cards of the Minor Arcana. Some are numbered, while others are people (Page, Knight, Queen, and King).

At the beginning of each section of interpretations, I'll remind you of these associations again, and go more into depth of what they mean. But for now, here's a very brief summary of the meanings of each suit:

- **Cups/Water/Emotions:** These cards all deal with creativity, passion, feelings, the heart, inspiration, and intuition. They also often have associations with the arts, especially music and theatre.
- **Swords/Air/Intellect:** These are all associated with thought, ideas, the mind, and also with the way we communicate with each other. They also sometimes refer to technology, science, and especially the written arts.
- **Pentacles/Earth/Body:** The Pentacles (sometimes called "Coins" in some Tarots) relate to the literal earth, our physical existence, our body, and other material aspects. This means they also are associated with wealth and health, and also with sport and any kind of manual work.
- **Wands/Fire/Will:** Wands (sometimes also called "rods" or "staves") speak to our sense of self and the way we influence the world, and wands are also associated with spirit (like when someone says they had a "spirited discussion.") They are also associated with charm, personality, enchantment, politics and power, and movement arts, especially dance or martial arts.

The Cycles of the Tarot

Don't stress too much about all those specific associations yet, because I want to first show you a really simple trick to understanding this logic: everything is a cycle.

First of all, the Major Arcana is a cycle. It starts at 0 with The Fool and then ends at 21 with The World. Each card along the way is like a stop in a journey, and each one shows you something about life. Also, the entire cycle repeats throughout our life, just like seasons repeat every year.

There are more cycles, too. The numbered cards of each suit in the Minor Arcana are also cycles, from ace (one) to ten. Those repeat throughout life, too, and are more like stages of development rather than stages of life.

And the court cards of each suit are also cycles, from pages to kings. These represent modes of being in the world, and we cycle through these just as often as any of the other cycles.

Each of these cycles will make a lot more sense once you start reading the cards, but here's an overview of these cycles.

The Cycle of the Major Arcana

The easiest way to understand the cycle of the Major Arcana is to lay out all the cards, from The Fool to The World, on the floor in a circle. And then, think of this circle as a kind of wheel that is constantly turning, and you are riding that wheel through life.

Or, you can think of it a lot like a Ferris Wheel, with each of those cards a position on the wheel. Except in this case, the cards aren't turning around the circle, you are, and in each place you get a different view of the world around you.

There are other ways of understanding this. For instance, some like to think about the way the zodiac appears to move across the sky because of the earth's orbit and rotation. In astrology, the positions of planets in those twelve signs have special influences on our lives, and as they move, those influences change as well.

But I find the absolute best way to understand this cycle is to just read the card interpretations one after another. By doing so, you can then see how certain cards proceed into other ones the way a clock hand moves around the clock. The important thing here, though, is to remember that the cycle keeps going. It's not a line from The Fool to The World, but rather a constantly turning cycle that keeps returning to The Fool.

Oh, and The Fool is you. So is The World. And so is every other card in the cycle, all at different times, repeating over and over again.

The Cycle of the Numbered Minor Arcana

Each suit of numbered cards tells a story of procession, from ace to ten. The aces are the beginning of that story, and the ten is its completion.

Each number along the way corresponds to a certain degree of development or a kind of challenge. Each card builds on all the numbers before it, either resolving a challenge from the previous one or adding a new one to be resolved in the next card. Think of each card as an alternating stitch in a seam, or the way that each step we take while walking is balanced by the next and the previous one.

Also, the numbers are neither good nor bad, and higher numbers aren't better than lower numbers. Think of them like seasons or like months, and you'll get a better idea of what I mean here.

Each number has certain basic associations that help you understand the meaning of the card. Don't worry about memorizing these or understanding them very deeply right now. I'll remind you of these in many of the interpretations of the cards, as well:

- **Aces:** These are the beginning of the cycle, the earliest stage where everything feels fresh, exciting, and also unknown.
- **Twos:** These are the moment our initial understanding and excitement interacts with the world. There's a tension inherent to this, but it is the kind of tension that spurs growth.
- **Threes:** Threes represent a kind of expansion that helps things manifest. A good way of thinking about this is to remember that it takes three points to define a plane in geometry, or how threes were a sacred number in Christianity, Celtic paganism, and many other spiritual beliefs.
- **Fours:** Fours represent structure, like the four walls of a house. Often, there is a kind of pause involved in fours, a necessary period of rest after a lot of growth.
- **Fives:** These are very often seen as negative because of the crisis each represents. No one likes crisis, of course, and yet without the kinds of situations the fives represent, we will never grow.
- **Six:** Sixes are really nice cards, primarily because they speak to the period of growth and the success that comes after we face and resolve the crisis of the fives.
- **Sevens:** The esoteric meaning of the sevens is that they represent the introduction of the spiritual or external into the six earthly planes. A

simpler way of putting this is that they're what happens when an unknown complicates everything we thought we knew.

- **Eights:** Eights are associated with harvest and spiritual structure. That's because they are the double of fours, and they are what happens when we integrate the unknown into our life.
- **Nines:** Nines represent a kind of completion, but with a mystery to it. A good way of understanding this is that they are the limit of human striving, which makes them the final challenge in the cycle.
- **Tens:** Tens are the true completion of the cycle, but also where the need for the cycle to begin again appears. In the famous image of the ouroboros, the snake eating its own tail, the ten would be right where the tail enters the snake's mouth.

The Cycle of the Court Cards

Each suit has four court cards, making a total of sixteen of them. In some forms of Tarot readings, the court cards are said to represent actual people in a person's life. In other versions, the person who the reading is done for is asked to pick one of these cards to represent themselves, and then take it out of the deck before the reading. But, I don't read Tarot this way, as it's never made much sense to me.

Instead, I've found it most helpful to see each court card in a suit as a mode of being in the world, and we cycle through these modes very often throughout life. Sometimes, the Queen of Wands might describe my life the best, while other times the Knight of Wands might. And none of these are good or bad. They all have really positive aspects, but also drawbacks, and I describe both in the interpretations later in this book.

Now, here is the way the cycle works for each suit of court cards:

- **Pages:** This is a kind of innocence, and an enthusiastic approach to things, much like a child going to school on the first day. It's also like the first few days of a new relationship, or a project, or a new way of seeing the world. In such stages, we don't fully understand the scope of a situation, but we've definitely got the enthusiasm we'll need for it.
- **Knights:** The knights know more than the pages, but they still don't know everything. Still, there's a strong drive in these cards, the kind that comes when you've chosen a direction and decided to head that way. Doesn't actually mean you know where you're going yet, of course.

- **Queens:** If the pages and knights are a bit immature, the queens are the early stages of maturity. There's a knowing confidence in these cards (as opposed to the baseless confidence of the knights). They represent a stage of development when we don't need to "prove ourselves" to anyone except ourselves.
- **Kings:** The Kings represent the fully-confident understanding of the suit in question. Think of a deeply-rooted mighty oak that supports an entire ecosystem. But of course, that oak isn't going anywhere, which is why the cycle then proceeds back to the pages again.

Some Extra Notes

Before I go any further, I need to clarify two things for you. They're both really important to understand if this guide is going to be useful for you.

Why No Reversed Cards?

You'll see that I don't include interpretations for reversed cards. That's because I don't read reversed cards anymore.

I once did. In fact, during the first fifteen years of reading Tarot, I always used them. But then I tried not using them, and suddenly my relationship to Tarot got immensely better.

This isn't to say that I don't think you should use reversed cards in your readings. They can definitely be helpful, or so I've heard. I never really found this to be the case. And anyway, like I said, in just a three card spread, using only upright cards, there are 456,456 possible card combinations. For context, there are somewhere between 500,000 and 1 million words in English, and only between 60,000 and 130,000 words in the French language. So, adding more possible card combinations through reversals is really just information overload.

Still, if you really feel like you want to use reversals in your readings, I'd suggest considering them as "minor" or "diminished" cards. In other words, a reversed card has a lesser influence on you or the situation than an upright card. How much less is up to your interpretation, of course. But again, you can really make this all much simpler and clearer for yourself by just using upright cards.

Why Is There So Much Gender in Tarot?

Many of the cards in Tarot are gendered because of its roots in medieval occult theories, as well as Arabic and Hermetic alchemists.

In their way of seeing the world, there are two primary forces — the feminine and the masculine —that make up everything in the world. Men and women each are composed of these forces, but not equally. Men tended to have more masculine force, while women tended to have more feminine force. And one of the goals of those occultists and alchemists was to reach a point where those forces were actually equal within them.

That point had a name: the "alchemical marriage," and this can also be seen running through the procession of cards in the Major Arcana. That's why there are so many alternating gendered cards (for example, Emperor/Empress, High Priestess/High Priest), and also why these cards seem to represent opposites or complements of each other.

Certain, this isn't the way everyone sees gender now, nor is it the way every society in the past has seen it. And for some, the feminine and masculine polarity running through the Tarot can feel uncomfortable.

There are certainly some newer versions of the Tarot that remove these polarities, and these may be quite useful for some people. Many of the interpretations of the cards in this guide would also still apply, though it might also be helpful to use a guide written specifically for these special kinds of Tarots.

However, even if the polarities don't reflect your actual view of the world, the mystery of the alchemical marriage running throughout the Tarot still has a lot to offer. Remember, for the alchemists, the feminine and masculine principles were both equal forces which run through all of life. This is similar to the way that many Asian cultures understand things, with two equal and complementary principles (for instance, *yin* and *yang*) responsible for our health and well-being, and these principles are often identified with the feminine and the masculine.

In other words, the Tarot actually presents a much more radical and less Western conception of gender than it first appears. This is seen especially in the court cards, where the queens can represent our current mode of living even though we are male, or the kings even though we are female. We are both the kings and the queens many times throughout our lives, and seeing ourselves this way can be quite liberating.

Part Two:
A Guide to the Cards

The Wands: the Path of Fire and Will

Cards in the suit of wands each relate to some aspect of the vital fire within all living things. Some call this fire "spirit," and see it as something which inhabits us while we live and then departs when we die. Many occultists and philosophers have instead associated this fire with "will," and see it more like a constant act of becoming.

Both ways of understanding this have much to offer, but there's an even simpler way of understanding it. I find that meditating on the power of fire itself — in all its creative and destructive potentials — teaches us a lot about this vital fire.

We use fire to transform substances. Cooking and baking are an obvious example, as are the larger fires of iron foundries. Stars themselves are fires, and the immense heat within them transforms elements into other ones. These same transformations occur through our own being in the world as well. When we act, we create, we change, we shape. And yes, we also destroy.

The cycle of the wands is the cycle of understanding this transformative fire within us. Through it, we understand our agency and the way we shape our lives and those of others. The wands are about creation (as opposed to creativity, which is more cups), power and leadership (whether political or personal), and especially about the "spark" in our lives that then spreads to others.

Thinking about the following questions may help when trying to understand their meanings in your readings:

- What do you intend for yourself and the world around you?
- What are you willing to do to make your life your own?
- What are the roles and costs of leadership and responsibility?
- How can we use our power without abusing it?

Ace of Wands

As with every Ace, this is a great card to find in a reading if you need something new in your life. Especially if you've felt a bit stuck, bored, or feel like the passion has drained out of your life, the Ace of Wands suggests a new fire is being kindled within you.

"Kindling" is a great way of understanding this card. If you've ever built a fire outdoors, you'll know you cannot just expect a large piece of wood to catch flame. Instead, you have to start with very small pieces of wood, dry leaves, sawdust, and other thinner materials. Once those catch flame, the heat they generate can then make the larger pieces of wood catch fire, too.

So, you can think of the Ace of Wands like the initial flame that ignites the kindling you've gathered, and it's also that flame as it jumps from leaf to leaf and twig to twig.

No, it's not a roaring fire yet. There's plenty of work to do to get this new thing — whatever it is — to the place you'd like it to be. But, most of that work will involve creating the best circumstances for it, rather than applying brute effort. If you've ever tried to re-arrange the wood of a fire before it's really started, you'll know that you can accidentally put the whole thing out that way.

So, whatever the thing is to which the Ace of Wands is referring, treat it like the beginnings of a fire. Make space for it, tend it, give it the right conditions, but don't try to meddle too early. Sometimes we get ahead of ourselves, "counting our chickens before they hatch." Talking too much about an early project can sometimes disperse all its initial energy, just like piling a large amount of wood on a tiny fire can smother it.

Instead of a new project, this card could be suggesting the beginning of a way of being in the world, especially around others. Perhaps a new vitality, a new burst of energy and self-confidence, a new thirst for life, a new sense of direction, even the early cultivation of leadership skills. Or, maybe a positive shift in a relationship, initiated through having a clearer sense of what you'd like or daring a moment of bold expression.

In present or future positions, it's best to ride the excitement that is here or is coming. The Ace of Wands in a past position, though, might suggest it's time to stop relying on that excitement, and instead start making it happen.

Two of Wands

Twos complicate the one in spectacularly unexpected ways, and this is especially true for the Two of Wands.

Often, this card is a reminder that a desire to do something is not actually enough to actually accomplish it. Sure, you might have a great idea for a project or a new business, or you might have all the drive you need to make radical changes in your life. But like a New Year's resolution to go to the gym or to change your eating habits, it's quite common to give up when we first realize it's not as easy as we assumed it would be.

That moment when your goals don't immediately manifest can be quite crushing. But the Two of Wands is telling you not to give up, and is also pointing to a deep transformation of will that will get you where you want to be. It especially asks you: what do you truly want, and who do you truly want to be? And what are you willing to do to get there?

That's why most renditions of this card show a figure looking out from a tower over distant lands, sometimes holding the world in his hand. There's a sense of both contemplation and longing in these depictions, introspection mixed with an awareness of how big the world really is.

Often the figure is standing between two wands, as if they are a doorway. This is another important sense of this card, the opening of the door between the self and the world. You may have suddenly found new horizons opened up to you, or have realized you need to broaden your perspective.

If the Ace of Wands is like the kindling of a fire, the Two of Wands is like the moment that fire is hot enough to do something with it. Now might be a time to think deeply about what you plan to do, where you want to go, and what else might be possible with this fire within you. Or maybe you need to gather more fuel for that fire so it can keep burning brightly.

In a past or present position, this card can occasionally suggest you should recommit to your goals, especially if your courage has faltered a bit after initial setbacks. Though some obstacles are truly impossible, most are really just initial challenges you can overcome with a little more perseverance. Try not to lose sight of where you want to go and who you want to be, even if things get a little tough. Also in a present position, and especially in a future one, this card can be suggesting you broaden your perspective about what is truly possible, and maybe even dare a little more.

Three of Wands

Threes resolve the tension of the twos, and the Three of Wands means you've overcome the initial difficulty implied in the Two of Wands. Having realized that you need more than intention and desire to make sustained changes or to manifest your visions in your life, you've now made the initial efforts and are beginning to see the results.

Beginners starting a weight lifting program benefit from a strange phenomenon that often makes long-term lifters quite jealous. "Newbies" can often gain twice or even three times more muscle in their first few months than experienced lifters can. That's because the body responds faster to stress it hasn't experienced before than it does to stress it's more familiar with.

That early bump is quite exhilarating, and it also occurs for many other things outside the gym. And this kind of early acceleration is what the Three of Wands is all about. You may be riding an early wave or experiencing a burst of energy and optimism that seems to bless everything you do. No, it won't last, but if you embrace the advantage it is giving you, you'll have the resources you need to build your dreams.

The excitement generated around a new project and the early successes you experience when you apply your will are very much like a favorable wind. When it fills your sails, it's best to let it take you as far as it can. But because the Wands are all about will, it's vital that you remember who is ultimately responsible for setting those sails and choosing the direction: *you are.*

In a past position, this card could be indicating that the cycle of early results has finished, and it's important for you to focus now on long-term planning and building sustainable habits that will carry you over during less favorable times. In a present position, embrace this fortunate moment of vitality and excitement, but remember it's only one part of a larger cycle. Take what you experience now and let it lead you where you'd like to go. And in a future position, such a moment is arriving, and you may want to seriously consider making an effort to expand your horizons, explore new places, encounter new ideas, and meet new people. These are the kinds of things that can put you in a better position to catch those favorable winds.

Four of Wands

The Four of Wands is all about celebration and the kind of joy that comes from the abundance we cultivate in our lives. When we delight in beauty, everything around us becomes more beautiful. When we choose enjoyment, our lives become much more enjoyable. And when we look at what we have already accomplished with a sense of gratitude and wonder, even the simplest things become cause for great celebration.

Most versions of this card show four upright staves strung with vines and fruits. There's both a sense of harvest and also of open-air ceremonies, like late-summer festivals or outdoor wedding receptions. Fours signify structure, and the Four of Wands reminds that not every structure needs to have solid walls for you to feel at home in it. We can feel secure and confident anywhere in the world, because our will connects us to others in powerful ways.

A crucial way we learn to see this connection is through conscious rituals. Much like setting up a tent, we can create intentional spaces in time and place where we tell the stories of our lives and listen to those of others. Birthday parties, anniversary celebrations, baby showers, weddings or hand-fastings, graduations, and funerals are all such rituals, as are occasional events like dinner parties, picnics, and family reunions. These all help us understand our place in the world and the importance of our relationships to each other.

This card might be suggesting you throw such a party, or accept the invitation to one, or it might also be urging you to mark an important success in your own life in some conscious way. However you choose to do so, don't be afraid to make it beautiful.

Especially, this card is a sign that you can relax a bit. The kindled spark of the Ace of Wands is now a stable hearth fire, and you can let it warm your soul. If you've been working hard on a project or spending a lot of time trying to put yourself "out there," take some time to enjoy what you've already done, and especially to enjoy this with other people. In other words: go play now.

It's a great card to receive in any position. In a past position, it sometimes also suggests you should focus on building upon what you already have accomplished, rather than starting new things.

Five of Wands

Five figures appear to be engaged in combat, with none of them stronger than the other. And, though there's certainly a sense that they are in aggressive combat, it's hard to ignore the suspicion they might also be engaged in a form of play.

Fives are transformations, crises, and paradoxes, and the Five of Wands represents the moments in life when we learn that having an effective argument, sufficient strength, a coherent moral stance, or a really great idea isn't enough to convince others, to change their minds, or to alter their behavior. Feeling we are "right" doesn't actually get us very far, nor does having the best intentions.

Despite all our careful planning and reasoning, we can only account for so much. Our perspectives will always be limited by the boundaries of our own experiences, our education, and our social relationships, and there will always be things we don't know or understand.

The Five of Wands is a good card to receive in a reading if you're due for a dose of humility, or if you feel like you've been hitting your head against a wall instead of moving forward on a project or towards a goal. Also, if you've recently been in an argument with someone you care about and no resolution seemed possible, this card is telling you what you need to do.

The fact that the figures in this card are often depicted as young men rather than soldiers is a signal about the kind of conflict this card is speaking about. Rather than war, it's a form of play. Especially if you tend to fear conflict or, on the other hand, take conflict too seriously, think on how in even the most aggressive team sports, a knocked-down player is often helped back up by the very same opponent who knocked him down.

In all positions, it's pointing to the limits of our will, and especially the need to understand the relationship between "self" and "other." By engaging with others and trying to see things their way — no matter how wrong we think they are — we learn something crucial about ourselves.

If this is referring to a time of conflict or interpersonal trouble, keep in mind the sense of playful competition or creative conflict in this card, especially if you are still struggling over a previous conflict. In a future position, it could be a gentle warning that your ego might need to be taken down a notch or two; and also in a future or present position, that you need to make a real effort to understand others' concerns or needs.

Six of Wands

The Six of Wands shows a figure astride a horse, holding a staff adorned with a laurel wreath. Often in the background are others on foot, accompanying or following the main figure.

Laurel wreaths are an ancient symbol of victory and the recognition of success, which is often why stylized laurel branches are used in the icons for prestigious awards. That's why the wreath is there in this card, too — you've succeeded in something, or are about to.

What specific kind of success this card refers to is probably described in the other cards in the reading, but you likely already know what it is. That's because the Six of Wands isn't just about external recognition, but also about the inner confidence we experience when our desire and will are aligned with our emotions, our intellect, our bodies, and the actions we take.

The conflict implied in the Five of Wands has now been resolved into a will that takes others into account. You may have recently learned how to pursue your goals in a way that also benefits others, or are about to realize how to do this. Maybe others have become truly interested in your project, your idea, or your plan, and they now offer to help you make it happen.

This card is often associated with leadership. Rather than "natural" leadership skills or leading by power, however, the Six of Wands refers to the kind of leadership that comes through mastering our will in relationship to the world. There's a sense in this card of taking many more things into account than just what we want, weighing these varied desires together, and then choosing the best direction in which to go.

There's also a sense of internal mastery and self-integration in the Six of Wands. It's a great card to receive if you are wondering if the study, discipline, or postponement of immediate pleasure required to reach a goal will be worth it. It could also be calling your attention to something in your life where you've already started on such a path or have mastered something you didn't realize you had.

It's a really positive card in present and future positions, especially if you keep in mind that "success" isn't always what society tells us it is. In a past position, it's also quite positive, with the additional sense that you might have overlooked an important victory in your life, or that it's time to recognize how much you've overcome to get to this present moment.

Seven of Wands

Sevens denote the arrival of an external obstacle, an unknown, or a cosmic or divine test into our lives. In such moments, our actions take on more significance than we initially imagined. And since the wands refer to the development of will, the Seven of Wands means we've attracted some real attention and our decisions have even more profound consequences.

Refining our will and becoming the kind of person we truly desire to be inevitably causes strife. This kind of strife isn't just the playful competition depicted in the Five of Wands, but truly difficult conflict, leading to the potential for real hurt and pain. Especially if we've surrounded ourselves with people who are not passionate about the same kinds of things we are, the changes we make in our own lives can feel like betrayals to them.

The Seven of Wands is the sudden appearance or recognition of these kinds of situations. Oftentimes we are caught unaware and had no way of predicting other people's reactions. And though this card suggests that we have a good vantage from which to defend ourselves, it doesn't necessarily mean we must.

Sometimes, criticism from others isn't actually helpful or even true, and sometimes we need to go our own way even in the face of social disapproval. This is especially important to keep in mind if you've often found yourself too reliant on the praise of others to determine the merit of your work, or if you rely too heavily on others for your sense of self-worth. When we do these things, we give other people power over our lives.

The arrival of this card in a reading is generally quite positive, but with some important caveats. If it's in a past position, it means the feeling of being judged by others or needing to fight for what you want and need is passing, but it may also be reminding you to stop dwelling on external disapproval. In a present position, you're in such a moment. You're going to be just fine. Don't worry, and don't let the experience make you bitter or vindictive. And in a future position, it might be telling you that a decision you are considering won't be popular with others or will elicit negative reactions. That doesn't mean you shouldn't go ahead with it, though. Consider this card's warning as an opportunity to think even deeper into your own motives and reasons.

Eight of Wands

Remember the "fortunate winds" of the Three of Wands? The winds blowing in the Eight of Wands are a much stronger gale, and you've gotten much better at sailing.

The Eight of Wands is a card of synchronicity and speed, as well as the intense energy that comes when you have freed yourself from the burdens and false beliefs placed upon you by others. The test of the Seven of Wands is complete, and you've now refined your will to such a point that it feels as if the entire cosmos is working with you.

Especially if this refers to a creative or business project, this card can point to a sense of a clear mission and what others might almost see as divine favor. Your charisma (see the Queen of Wands) is at its peak, and as long as you direct your energy fully towards a goal — rather than wasting it on distractions — your actions will have profound effects.

The sense of speed implied in this card can be a bit disconcerting, though. There may be an urgency to decisions, short windows in which to seize opportunities, and very little room for considering all your options.

If this feels true of your current situation, and especially if you are feeling pressured to act when you're not fully prepared, remember everything you've already learned. You've accumulated all the skills and the self-understanding to make the correct decisions in this situation, and this is absolutely not the time for self-doubt.

What is written here applies equally for present and future positions in readings, but with future positions you may find it's a good idea to tie up loose ends or finish the groundwork for something nearing completion.

In a past position, you may be just coming out of such a period and are now surveying where these decisions have led you. It's especially important not to indulge in regret or could-have-beens at this point. That forward movement would have propelled you here no matter what.

Nine of Wands

In the Nine of Wands, a vigilant warrior, bearing a bandage on a wounded head, holds a staff in front of a line of staves forming a fence. Unlike with the more clearly positive imagery of the Nine of Cups or Nine of Pentacles, things don't seem so optimistic in this card.

Look again, though, and you might notice how — despite being wounded and tired — the warrior is equally alert and also at rest. He's certainly been through a lot, but he hasn't given up. Also, though it might seem he is holding a staff in preparation for battle, he is also using it for support.

In any truly worthwhile endeavor, there will be countless setbacks, epic hurdles, and moments of extreme exhaustion. In fact, if we ever really knew how difficult something would be, we probably never would have started. The thing is, we ourselves get stronger, more skilled, and more resilient along the way, and by the time those challenges arrive, we're in a place where we can better face them.

Often this card arrives at times when you thought something was already settled, but yet another challenge has come or another obstacle is in your way. You might feel exhausted or ready to quit, even though you've already come so far. And you might even feel irritated, wondering why you still need to deal with the same kinds of problems as before.

There's also another meaning possible. The wands are about refining the will, and about saying "yes" to the challenges and opportunities of life. Even more difficult, though, is learning to say "no."

You may need to finally cut someone or something out of your life, or to create a much stronger boundary between yourself and those who unnecessarily demand your attention. The family or friends of addicts will know too well how hard it can be to do this, but also how not doing so helps prevent the necessary crises that lead to change. The key to this, and also a deeper truth to this card, is remembering that the work to become yourself is something anyone is capable of. You do not need to make excuses for others, and you cannot do that work for them.

This card in a past position can be similar to the meaning of the Seven of Wands, with an extra emphasis on not being defined by your past struggles. In a present or future position, the need to create boundaries and simplify your life can be especially important, depending on other cards that appear.

Ten of Wands

In this card, a figure seems to struggle under the weight of carrying ten large staves to their final destination. Sometimes, this figure is shown as quite old, while in others it's a youth. Many interpretations of the Ten of Wands point to the immediate sense of burden and overwhelm apparent in this card. However, the tens point to moments of completion in which a new beginning is implied, so it's important not to focus too much on the apparent negative aspects in the illustrations.

The Ten of Wands usually appears in readings when it's time to reflect on where you've been, how far you've come, and what more there is to life. It asks several questions: what comes next? What has all this struggle really been for? And once you've succeeded, will you truly be yourself?

It's dangerous to derive too much of our sense of who we are from the things we accomplish. When this happens, we can then struggle to finish or to pass off leadership to someone else — we worry we will lose a source of meaning and self-worth. Especially, it can become difficult to rest or to take breaks, which can then lead to illness and burnout.

Though the Ten of Wands comes with a warning about over-identifying with our accomplishments, it also proclaims an assurance and a promise. You've done what you needed to do, and you don't need to work so hard. For example, a mother worrying over her children might take this card as a sign that it's time to let them worry about themselves, instead. For a leader of a group or organization, this card could be a reminder to delegate responsibility to others.

In a past position, the Ten of Wands might ask you to remember earlier situations where you identified too much with *doing* instead of *being*, or that you are now experiencing the consequences of that tendency. In a present position, take a real moment (maybe a vacation?) to step back and evaluate your work and life goals. And in a future position, you're almost done or almost at your limit — start asking what comes next and what you can pass off to others.

Page of Wands

My favorite illustration for this card shows a young child playing with a stick. Perhaps you remember doing exactly such a thing as a child, waving around a wand to transform your friends or your surroundings into magical beasts, or pretending you were fighting off fierce enemies with a staff to save the world or to reach some powerful treasure. If you can summon such memories into your consciousness, you will have everything you need to understand what the Page of Wands teaches.

The Page of Wands represents these childlike moments in the development of our will, no matter our age. They are moments when we become aware of what can be, and how we hold in our hands the power to make those things occur. Of course, we don't actually know how do to this yet, but what is most important here is the sense of wonder and awe at the possibilities themselves.

There's a subtle second meaning to the phrase, "make-believe" that fits the Page of Wands very well. We generally think of make-believe as something only children do, yet this is also something we all do. Some people's entire careers (advertisers, marketers, preachers, politicians) are devoted to making people believe some things are true and other things are not, and the power they wield is often a misuse of the will that the suit of wands symbolizes.

The Page of Wands is the power of make-believe in all its innocence and playfulness. It's the dawning awareness of what the will is capable of, without any of the negative senses of adult manipulation and power struggles.

Whatever its position, this card might appear when you need to reconnect to these earlier moments of playful possibility, or also when you need to be aware of how the will of others shapes your own circumstances and sense of limits. It can just as easily be a call to return to the enthusiasm and wonder of innocence, or to beware of being manipulated by others. Both the negative and positive possibilities stem from the same root, which is the sacred power in each of us to shape our own lives.

Knight of Wands

I first really understood the Knight of Wands when I started mountain hiking. I'm quite terrified of heights, and I'm also quite clumsy, and both of these facts together would make crossing rivers gorges or other obstacles very frightening. I then learned the best way to deal with these places was to throw my backpack to the other side first. Since I needed everything in that pack, I would then have no choice but to find some way across.

Sometimes we need to act without knowing what the result will be or even how we will get there. Sometimes we need to do things that significantly shake up some part of our life in ways we cannot predict. Sometimes, impatience and recklessness are essential to becoming who we want to be and doing what we want to do.

The Knight of Wands is exactly those kinds of moments, and the actions which get us to where we want to go. It represents will as an impetuous power that is not yet tempered by training, discipline, or practice. It's the impatient spark that lights a fire without caring whether or not there's enough fuel to sustain it later. It's taking risks: signing up for a gym membership, asking someone out on a date, applying for a new job, buying a one-way ticket to a place you've never been before, purposefully leaving your phone at home, starting a course.

No. You don't know what will happen, or if the risk will even result in anything better. You might face rejection, or failure, but the Knight of Wands reminds you that nothing will ever happen unless you take risks.

When the Knight of Wands appears in a present or future position, I find it most helpful to think about all the truly transformative actions in my life, many of which could just as easily have been called foolish. If I had truly known the risks, I might never have acted. And maybe there is somewhere in my life I need that kind of energy again.

It's also possible that its appearance in a past position is asking us to take responsibility for a situation we caused, regardless if we were actually aware we were causing this. Recognizing the unintended consequences of our actions is a very important phase of transitioning from an adolescent to an adult.

Queen of Wands

If the Queen of Wands were a person, she'd be an elegant and charming host who has thrown a large party for a varied group of guests who do not know each other well. She walks gracefully from room to room and from person and person, speaking to each in a way that makes them feel as if they are the most interesting person in the world. And when she then speaks to the next guest, there's no jealousy, because everyone feels more generous and connected to each other because of her.

The Queen of Wands represents the power of self-confidence that leads us not to compete but rather to connect with others. It's the boldness of a lover who is not held back by fear or shame, whose self-assuredness invites us to be bold and self-assured, too.

There's a contagious quality to the kind of charisma the Queen of Wands represents. When we are most ourselves, others around us find it easier to be themselves, too. When we stop asking for permission to be what we want to be or making apologies for taking up too much space in the world, the fire in us also sparks fires in others.

If you've had difficulties embracing your will and spirit in such a way, think about the way fire seems to "dance" as it burns, or the way a dancer doesn't seem to think about the steps as she dances. Movement is a recurring theme in the suit of Wands, and finding new ways to express the movement of your will through the body or through place can be a very useful method of opening up places where your sense of self has become stagnant or blocked.

Because the appearance of this card represents the opposite of jealousy, bitterness, and comparison, it might actually be beneficial to ask yourself if any of those traits are currently affecting your life. Often, we can resent the self-assuredness of others, rather than learning from them how to be more self-assured as well.

Most often, this card appears as a call to inhabit yourself more fully and to avoid self-doubt. If you have had the sense others are looking at you in judgment, you might have misinterpreted their gaze through negative filters. Or, if there are opportunities you may be turning down out of a fear of not being enough, imagine what the Queen of Wands would say to such a fear, and realize you are also her.

King of Wands

The King of Wands is what we might call a true king, a leader of people through vision and will, rather than through force, manipulation, violence, or baseless claims of authority.

Though we rarely — if ever — see such kings in history, there is a mythic sense in us that such figures have existed or can exist. That's because we experience many moments in our lives when this kind of leadership flows through us or through those around us.

The King of Wands represents full confidence in the direction you are heading and the inevitability of your destination. There's no sense of struggle or conflict implied in such confidence. It's as if everyone around you immediately recognizes your goals, offers their support, and sees in your direction something that will benefit many others as well.

Like all the other court cards, this card is only one aspect of our humanity. In other words, it's not a permanent state, and that's also a good thing. There's a danger in trying to hold on too long to king aspects, and the danger in the King of Wands is the abdication of our own will to those of others or the possibility of becoming trapped in a leadership role we cannot sustain.

Will is like fire, a powerful force that can burn brightly but then also burn out. People in leadership roles can often lose connection to the passion that initially propelled them to those positions, and the independent spirit of the wands doesn't mix very well with the burdens and obligations that others place on them.

If this card has shown up in a past position, give some attention to ways in which your long-term vision may have gotten clouded by obstacles, obligations, or even too much success in a short period of time. Reconnecting to the playfulness of the Page of Wands might help set you back on track.

In a present position, ask if there are specific roles you need to take on that will further your sense of self in collaboration with others. Maybe people are offering you support in ways you've mistaken for indifference, or they are more willing to accept who you are than you've assumed.

This card is especially positive in a future position, often suggesting that your actions now will be recognized and appreciated by others, or that you'll soon settle an internal indecisiveness that is holding you back.

The Pentacles: The Path of Earth and the Body

The Pentacles speak to our existence as bodies, and also the material basis of our lives. And though traditional interpretations of these cards usually focus on money as a symbol of wealth, a much better way of understanding them is that they refer to physical abundance in all its forms.

Health, for example, is one such physical abundance. When we are in great health, it feels like there is even more of us to go around. We can do more in life and be more present for others when we are feeling fully alive. When our health is diminished, things can feel quite the opposite.

The cycle of this suit is a path to developing our physical presence and abundance, no matter our age and current circumstances. This includes health and even wealth in its monetary forms, but what's most important here is the relationship between our physical efforts and that abundance.

That's why many of the cards in this suit refer to work. Work is the way we manifest ourselves into the earth and thus create abundance for ourselves and others. Not just official waged or salaried work, but also the too-often invisible kinds of work we do to make our homes beautiful, to sustain ourselves, and to care for those we love.

Thinking about the following questions may help when trying to understand their meanings in your readings:

- What is my relationship to my body, and how can I be more present?
- What kinds of abundance do I lack, and how can I cultivate more?
- How can I feel more at home in the world?
- What is truly "enough" for me?
- What do I do when I have more than I need?

Ace of Pentacles

With the Ace of Pentacles, we begin the cycle of deeper connection to the body and to our material existence, and like every other ace, there is an initial excitement or force that starts the cycle for us.

Traditionally, the Ace of Pentacles is said to refer to a financial windfall or a period of great health. It's also often seen as a sign that it's a great time to start a new job or business. It's all that, certainly, but if you focus only on the relationship of pentacles to monetary wealth, you'll miss out on their much deeper meaning and the greater promise of this card.

We've all had times when we feel particularly "at home" in our bodies, along with many more times when we feel the opposite. In those moments of connection, the artificial division between our mind and our body seems to disappear. It should, after all: the brain is literally an organ of the body, not some external presence.

This artificial division leads us to all kinds of problems in life, and not least of these is the way we often sacrifice our health and neglect caring for our bodies. We treat our bodies as if they are a raw resource to be exploited in exchange for wealth, just as the natural world is treated as raw material to be turned into profit.

The Ace of Pentacles is often pointing to a moment we reject those artificial divisions and remember what we are. In such moments, we feel present, rooted, and strong. We feel the weight of our physical existence and the inherent joy of our muscles moving us through the world. And especially, we feel the potential of our lives, and how much more we can live.

Money is often a symbol for that feeling of potential, and certainly having extra money can make you feel quite optimistic about what is possible. But being in great health, feeling particularly strong and at home in the body, and finding yourself deeply rooted in the place you live are more sustainable sources of that potential.

In a present position, consider the Ace of Pentacles a suggestion to plant the seed of something in your life. That could be better health, better finances, a long-term work project, or a more embodied way of living in the world. In a future position, it could be a sign that the present will lead to such a new practice. And as with all aces in past positions, the Ace of Pentacles here could be a suggestion to now cultivate what you started.

Two of Pentacles

The Two of Pentacles usually depicts a figure playfully juggling two coins with the symbol of infinity between them. Often behind the figure are ships navigating large waves, but none of them appear to be in real danger.

There are two lessons anyone starting a gym training program or sport learns quite quickly from experience. The first is that muscles must be used and strained in order to grow, and the second is that the actual growth of those muscles only occurs in the times when you aren't using those muscles and are instead resting.

Sure, this might initially seem like a paradox. But it's actually a core truth that applies to much more than just muscle gain. The alchemical formula *solve et coagula* describes this same idea. Substances must be broken down first before they can be reformed into new substances, and this process doesn't happen just once, but repeats infinitely throughout all of life.

Not long after you begin work on a project, a new health or fitness program, a new job, a business, or an embodied practice, you'll encounter moments of strain. If these experiences are new to you, you might be tempted to give up, or to worry that things will get too hard. But the Two of Pentacles reminds that these strains are essential to growth. In fact, as with lifting weights a little heavier than you're used to, resistance and tension are what actually lead you to become stronger.

This card might appear at times when you are feeling a bit stressed, or when you feel like you are having difficulty balancing work and rest. On the other hand, it could also appear at times you have been avoiding physical exertion or "putting yourself out there" because of a fear of effort involved. In either situation, the message is the same: tension is necessary for growth, and so is the rest after periods of strain. If you're leaning too much in one direction, try shifting to the other one, and do so with a sense of playfulness.

In a past position, this card's appearance might signify this time of juggling is over, or that an imbalance between tension and rest might have influenced your current situation. Elsewhere, the card is often a reminder to keep an eye on which side of the scales you're leaning into with this balancing act, and make sure to also lean the other way, too.

Three of Pentacles

Most of the work that we do in modern society often feels unrewarding. Many times, we take jobs not because we are really passionate about them, but because they are the only jobs available or because they will pay better than what we would really prefer to do. Especially, we often don't get to see the direct results of our work, nor do we get to benefit directly from those results.

This can all lead us to feel like work is a joyless and soulless activity, something we "have" to do instead of something we "want" to do. But this is only because our societies have such a limited idea of what work is. We are led to believe that the only work that has value is what we are paid to do, while all the other work we perform in our lives becomes invisible.

When you cook a dinner for yourself, your family, or your friends, that's work. When you read a book about something you care deeply about, that's also work. Caring for those around you, or for a garden, or for your body, is absolutely work. These kinds of work flow naturally from us, and they are often so rewarding that we don't even feel as if they require any effort.

The Three of Pentacles is about the feeling we get when we can see the results of our work and become excited about it. Sometimes, this can take the form of recognition from others at our jobs, or when someone remarks on the work we've done at the gym, or when a family member or friend thanks us for a meal we cooked. It's also possible that the recognition comes from within us, as when we delight in something we've just accomplished or take pride in the way we did something.

And this card is not just about the feeling we get from such recognition, but about the truth we learn about our own abilities and how they can create value, beauty, and joy in the world.

All of this applies regardless of the card's position. In a future position, the Three of Pentacles can also be an assurance that the results of the work you're doing now — whatever that work is — will benefit yourself and others. In a past position, it could be reminding you to take account of the results of your previous work. And in a present position, it can occasionally be a suggestion to hone certain skills through study, practice, training, or collaboration for the best results.

Four of Pentacles

So much attention is given to weight loss in social and other media, and body fat is often depicted as a symbol of laziness, sickness, and poverty. Because of all this, it's very easy to forget what body fat actually is, and how essential it is to human life.

Besides its crucial role in cushioning organs which would otherwise get damaged when we moved, fat is how our body stores the energy from food for later use. It's essentially the body's savings account, and the excess fat humans put on naturally just before winter is how our ancestors were able to survive times of food scarcity.

Now, certainly, we moderns are now often out of sync with the natural cycles of abundance and scarcity, and this doesn't just apply to body fat. We often borrow money on credit at times when we probably shouldn't be spending so much, or splurge on purchases without thinking about longer term consequences. And this isn't just a problem of individuals — entire nations borrow against uncertain futures and consume more than what the earth can sustainably provide.

Fours are structure, and the Four of Pentacles points to the necessity of structuring your resources to figure out if you have what you need. As with the entire suit, the resources to which it speaks could be financial, or it could refer to your health, or it could refer to your physical surroundings.

For finances, it might be suggesting you check over your bank accounts well and consider cutting back on expenses you don't need. Here, your focus should be on saving for later, "putting on fat for the winter" or "saving for a rainy day." For health, you might want to consider adjusting what you eat, getting more rest, or even getting a routine medical checkup if possible. And for your physical surroundings, there may be some repairs or maintenance you need to do on your home, even if that's only catching up on laundry, cleaning a neglected area, or decluttering a room. This advice applies especially if the card appears in a future position.

In a present position, it might also suggest you need to be more realistic and practical in a situation, rather than getting lost in possibilities. And in a past position, it can suggest that you've already accumulated what was needed or rested enough, and it's okay to spend some of that now.

Five of Pentacles

During the winter festival called Carnival — whose name comes from the Latin word for "meat" — people throughout Europe would feast for days on the best foods remaining from the autumn's harvest. It was one last great celebration before the hardest time of the year, a period of winter famine and hunger that the Catholic Church later ritualized as Lent.

To get a deep sense of what the Five of Pentacles is, imagine yourself a medieval peasant just before the end of winter. You now have almost nothing but boiled grains to eat, and the land outside is still so cold and barren that you're not sure spring will ever come. And worst of all, you still remember the feeling of fullness and the taste of all those rich Carnival foods, and this makes your current hunger even more unbearable.

That's the bodily feeling the Five of Pentacles speaks to, the raw fear of not having enough and the uncertainty of what you'll do next. This is why it's often interpreted as the "divorce" card, but not because it signifies an actual relationship breakup. Instead, it refers to the deep worry we experience when the life we've built up with others seems suddenly to crash down around us, and we don't know how we'll make it on our own.

Remember, fives are transformations, and the suffering implied in the fives is what initiates the necessary change we need. The initiation of the mystery for this card is usually a sense of physical loss. It can sometimes be an injury, an illness, or a sudden financial misfortune, but more often it seems to point to a general change in circumstances that causes us to make necessary changes, too.

In all positions, the Five of Pentacles can also point to the moments we notice we have become over-reliant (and sometimes even addicted) to someone or something, and are struggling to adjust to this knowledge. Someone you relied on may have just turned out to be unavailable or unreliable, or some way of doing things no longer gives you the results you hoped for. Learn from these situations, change what you can change, accept what you cannot, and remember that spring will always follow winter, no matter how far away you fear it is.

Six of Pentacles

One of the slogans of the Paris Commune is a phrase some people mistakenly believe comes from the Bible: "from each according to his ability, to each according to his need." And if there's a slogan for the Six of Pentacles, this would be it.

Sixes all have a sense of peaceful expansion, and you can think of them as the results of the difficult transformation implied in the fives. In the Five of Pentacles, we saw all the uncertainty and instability that comes with not having enough. In the Six of Pentacles, we now also see what is possible when we have more than we need.

This card is about conscious generosity and the kind of larger benefits such gifts create. And for this kind of generosity, we must know what would be truly most helpful.

Consider the simple act of helping an elderly woman take her groceries up the stairs to her apartment. The amount of effort we need for such an act is much less than the effort she would need, and so the gift of our extra time and strength has a profound effect for her. On the other hand, donating to a fundraiser or a political campaign might have much less effect, and that money we give might actually translate into a much larger portion of our time (through wages) than helping that woman.

Understanding the effects of our generosity is only possible when we have an embodied understanding of the way resources flow through us and what is truly needed. That understanding is what the Six of Pentacles points to, and its appearance may signal the arrival of this kind of awareness in your life or the need to embody that awareness.

Especially important in this card is the sense of human relationships and the way gifts strengthen them. You may be currently receiving such generosity from someone, and this card might be asking you to recognize this in some way. This especially applies for its appearance in a past position. In a present or future position, it might also be pointing to someone in your life who could really benefit from a conscious gift of time or resources that you currently have in abundance. Many friendships are made and deepened from seemingly minor acts of generosity.

Seven of Pentacles.

Anyone who gardens quickly learns a kind of humility about our roles and what we are actually doing. Though we often talk about how we are "growing" certain flowers or vegetables, we know this isn't true. We're not growing anything. The plants are doing the growing, and we're just helping them along their way.

Sevens are the entrance of an unknown or external understanding into the area of our lives the suits speak to, and the Seven of Pentacles is what happens when we begin to understand the role of nature in our health, wealth, and physical existence. When we grow the gardens of our lives, accumulate resources, increase our health, and work to exist fully-embodied on this earth, we are never doing this alone.

The further away our societies move from this understanding, the more problems we face. When processed foods replace whole grains and local vegetables, people become sick. When cities full of concrete replace wild lands, people become depressed. When we take from the earth without giving back to it, the soil becomes depleted and the environment ruined.

The Seven of Pentacles is a call to take into account the role of the natural processes in our lives, with a specific focus on the relationship between our actions and their effects. And when looking at these things, we must be as neutral and pragmatic as possible.

For instance, if you are currently experiencing poor health or poor finances, the arrival of this card might be suggesting you take sober account of how previous choices may have contributed to this situation, and how much might also be due to external reasons. This is also equally true if you're experiencing great health or a good financial situation.

If there is any fear that comes up in you around these issues, try to imagine you are both a gardener and also the garden being tended. Then, ask how you might best help your life grow.

In a past position, the matter of consequence is particularly important — the situation now has roots in previous actions. In a present position, you might benefit more from a hands-off approach to a situation, as the effort required is already put in. And in future positions, this card is traditionally seen as quite positive, a reminder that your current efforts will have particularly strong results.

Eight of Pentacles

While writing this book, I stacked all 78 tarot cards in a pile next to me and, starting with the Major Arcana, flipped over each card to write its interpretation. Sometimes, staring at the stack of remaining cards felt a bit overwhelming, and I worried that I would never finish. This worry actually slowed the writing, though, and I was forgetting the message of this card.

The Eight of Pentacles is the mystery of work, the deep bodily joy that springs from our efforts whenever we stop focusing on the hoped-for results. It's going to the gym, making a large and complicated dinner for friends, re-organizing a room, or taking on long projects not because you're hoping to get something out of these things, but instead because you really enjoy them.

When we do these kinds of work, time seems to stand still, and we feel fully present in ourselves and the world around us. We become fully engaged in the task before us, and we feel deeply alive. Much like catching a glimpse of a landscape so beautiful it seems to take our breaths away, nothing else except that moment and the beauty we experience seems to exist.

Such moments are rare in our lives. Often, we are constantly fidgeting, unfocused, unable to be fully present. Often, we waste more energy on procrastination than the amount of effort actually required to complete a task. And even when we find ourselves in deep moments of presence or great beauty, we often end them by pulling out our phones to take photos.

The Eight of Pentacles is a call to come back to the present, to your body, and to work before you. If you've found yourself overly worried about future results or the amount of work something requires, consider it a promise that it will all be worth the effort, but only if you actually put in that effort.

This card also sometimes refers to long-term training or the skills that come from applied effort. So, in a past position, it could also be a reminder to be more self-confident in the abilities you accumulated through experience or training. Maybe you are more capable than you believe.

And in a future position, it might be suggesting you should consider getting more skills through training or study, or apply your efforts to a much longer-term project than you are accustomed to.

Nine of Pentacles

The nines represent a final challenge in the cycle of development. In its swords version, that challenge is to move past self-imposed fears; in the wands version it's to not be defined by our struggles, and in the cups version, it's to not mistake pleasure as the final goal of desire.

To understand the challenge of the Nine of Pentacles, contemplate the imagery of the card and imagine yourself the woman in the beautiful walled garden. Everything you could possibly want is there, all of life is abundance, and you have everything you need.

Would such a situation on its own truly make you happy? Or would you perhaps become bored with it after a while, find yourself wondering what else there might be to life, maybe even sometimes miss the struggles of your past because they made you feel more alive?

The Nine of Pentacles is a gentle reminder that a thriving physical existence is a very strong foundation upon which to build our lives, but it is not life itself. It is possible to become so obsessed with fitness or avoiding illness that you miss out on experiencing life, or to spend so much time trying to accumulate wealth that you never actually really live. We need both that strong foundation — and also what we build upon it — to fully dwell on this earth.

One good way to embrace this challenge is to ask yourself the reasons why you strive for certain physical things, and to consider those answers as your true goals. For instance, if you struggling with poor health and want to be healthier, ask yourself what you would do if you were feeling better. If you are trying to find a higher paying job, ask yourself what you intend to do with that better income. Or if you are exercising heavily or dieting, try to ask what that's really for.

Despite this challenge, the appearance of this card is usually considered positive. It could be an indication you've reached a point where you can pursue those larger goals or just enjoy what you've already accomplished. There's a security and stability implied here — especially in present and future positions — that can give you space for contemplation. In a past position, it can also suggest a particular need to avoid isolation, or a worry about feeling too "old" to try to pursue something that truly excites you.

Ten of Pentacles

As part of the ritual of creating this book for you, I chose to write about this card after every other part of the book was written. That's because the Ten of Pentacles represents a manifestation of our material existence, but as the completion of the cycle of the pentacles, it also represents a letting go or a release of our work into the world.

That's why it's very often associated with legacies and inheritances, and specifically the things we pass along. It's about what we have gathered up along the way — be that material resources, skills, training, or the results of hard work — and then giving it to others.

Everything we do, everything we have, and everything we are is built upon the lives and work of others. Our ancestors gifted us not only the genetics which shape our bodies, but also a great wealth of knowledge passed down through everyday interactions which helped us become who we are. And we, too, pass this great wealth along to others in ways so subtle that we rarely notice how rich we all really are.

This is what the Ten of Pentacles teaches us. Whereas the challenge of the Nine of Pentacles is to understand that abundant physical existence is merely a foundation to life instead of its goal, the Ten of Pentacles answers that challenge by reminding us where that foundation actually comes from, and how it can never be destroyed.

If this card has shown up in your reading, think about all the ways in which you are made up of others, and they are made up of you. The earth is the great commons of all of life. It is the very ground of our being, and we are all its citizens, its children, and its caretakers. We never create alone, and we never create only for ourselves.

The Ten of Pentacles in a past position is very often pointing to an inheritance you have received. Occasionally, this can actually refer to a literal one, but even more often it's trying to draw your attention to something more enduring than just money. The same is true in a present position, with the sense that the moment you are in is especially guided by past legacies. Or, it can be suggesting that it's really time to release your work into the world, whatever that work is.

In a future position, it can sometimes be an encouragement to think more long-term about the current moment, and ask what legacy your current actions are building for others.

Page of Pentacles

Imagine a child thinking about all the things she can buy with her allowance, unconcerned with how little or much that really is. Also, imagine a child planting an acorn in the ground, dreaming of how big of an oak it will one day be and unconcerned with how long that would actually take.

Both of these examples represent something about the sense of awareness of the body and the physical world in the Page of Pentacles. Sure, there's certainly a kind of naivety involved in such acts, but as with the message of The Fool, we need this kind of innocence to even start something.

The Page of Pentacles is traditionally associated with students and study, and this can seem an odd relationship since the Pentacles are not about the intellect. However, this makes more sense when we keep in mind that studies are not always academic. In fact, for a very long time — and even still now — many professions were taught directly through apprenticeships rather than schools. In these situations, a youth learns directly from a more experienced person who teaches the student while working.

This mode of learning is quite common even outside of job skills. Many of us learn how to cook from our parents or how to play sports from those who already know the rules. What matters most in all these situations is our willingness to learn and our repeated physical practice of what we are being taught. We start out naive and ignorant, and then soon find the knowledge running through our very bodies.

When the Page of Pentacles shows up, you may be in the early stages of learning something, or you may have just become aware of some physical or material difficulty whose solution you cannot yet imagine. This could apply to a large project — building a house, getting out of debt, starting a course of study — or something more related to your body, such as trying to change eating or lifestyle habits, dealing with a disability, starting a training program, or bettering your health. In such cases, the Page of Pentacles is a great reminder that it's best to just start somewhere and not be too attached to desired outcomes. You'll learn what more is needed along the way.

Or it could be suggesting you need to go a bit deeper, develop your skills more consciously, or move beyond these initial stages.

Knight of Pentacles

There's a lot of hatred for the figure of the "jock." Usually depicted as young men, they're denigrated as ignorant and uneducated, too caught up in their physical existence to contemplate more complex things. Yet just as with other negative archetypes in society, there's an envy attached to this hatred. The strength, athleticism, and body confidence of a jock, and the way jocks appear to just act without worrying too much about the consequences, represent something that many of us feel we lack.

At the root of this is our modern false division between the body and the mind. We pretend as if our brains are not actually part of our bodies, and then believe we have to make a choice between being physical beings and pursuing more intellectual pursuits.

The Knight of Pentacles reminds us there is no such division, and we do not need to make these false choices. It represents a mode of engagement with the world that is available to all of us at any time in our life, no matter our degree of fitness, our health, or the capacities of our bodies.

Engaging with the world in this way can look like many things, and in all of these ways the key is a simple physical pleasure which our societies do not often value. Washing a sink full of dishes by hand can certainly seem boring, and yet the feeling when the last dish is dried and put away feels quite good. Going for a walk with no real destination in mind is another example: the enjoyment that comes from it can never be bought in a store. The same goes for more intense activities like weight lifting or sports, a day of difficult yet rewarding work, a long hike, or longer projects like a deep cleaning of your home or building a garden. What is most important in all this is your bodily engagement with the world, and the subtle pleasures which come from that engagement which remind you what life actually is.

The Knight of Pentacles is a reminder that your body is also who you are. It's through the body that you connect with the world around you, and also through the body that the world communicates with you. Be more body right now, and less thought. If there are situations you are avoiding because of the work involved, or if you are trying to distract yourself from chronic pain or poor health, you're making things harder than they need to be.

And sometimes, this card can be a gentle caution that you're too focused on your own bodily existence and are ignoring the health and well-being of your surroundings.

Queen of Pentacles

Whenever I see the Queen of Pentacles, I imagine a strong, hearty woman with a big body, a bigger laugh, a garden always full of vegetables, a kitchen full of drying herbs, and a dinner table that is always full of food.

The Queen of Pentacles is the ultimate "earth mother" card, representing a deep confidence in the abundance of the world and a secure understanding of the relationship between the earth, our health, and our wealth. It also represents all the work that we do for ourselves and others, the work that sustains and nurtures life.

Sure, these are certainly qualities typically associated with traditional housewives, and so this can seem too traditional for some people. But like all the court cards, this mode of being is one we all inhabit many times in our lives. And also, many men — myself included — take on roles in our relationships and our homes that fit these traditional descriptions.

Especially, there's a deep embodiment associated with this card, one that teaches us what is needed and how to meet those needs. When we are fully in our bodies, we are able to cultivate our own health and well-being. And it's from that abundance that we are better able to care for others.

In other words, there's no "sacrifice" implied in the Queen of Pentacles. This queen doesn't give up some of her time and resources to nurture others, but rather passes on the extra that she has created.

And though the pentacles are often mistakenly assumed to signify only monetary wealth, this card makes it quite evident they are about a different kind of wealth altogether. There's a strong practicality in the meaning of the Queen of Pentacles, and an appreciation for simple pleasures. It's a Friday evening spent at home taking a long bath rather than going out, or the subtle enjoyment of cooking a meal at home rather than going to an expensive restaurant. It's knowing what is truly valuable, rather than what society tells us is valuable.

The Queen of Pentacles is part of a cycle, though, and being too long in this mode (usually signified by the card being in a past position in readings) can lead us to become too focused on health and material well-being, or we can become overly-defined as a caregiver to others.

King of Pentacles

In the description of the Page of Pentacles, I suggested you imagine a child planting an acorn in the ground dreaming of how big of an oak it will one day be. The King of Pentacles is that oak.

Oaks fill an ecological niche called "keystone species." Beings in these roles hold an entire ecosystem together and shape it by their very presence. Even just one oak is able to sustain countless other animals and plants, providing food for squirrels, mice, and many kinds of birds, as well as providing shelter and safety to many others in their branches — and under those branches during storms. Their massive roots hold together soil that might otherwise erode, and on those roots grow countless kinds of fungi, including that rarest of mushrooms, the truffle.

Like oaks, the King of Pentacles represents a deeply-rooted physical presence that sustains others through its very existence. An oak doesn't need to try to provide for others, it just naturally does, and so does the mode of being represented by this card.

Physical strength is certainly one aspect of this kind of provision, as is material wealth. If you've ever needed to move something very heavy in your house, you'll know how much easier it is if you've a strong friend to rely on. Or, if some health catastrophe occurs, you'll know how much easier it is if you can rely on the financial help of someone else to get you through.

The King of Pentacles represents the times when we're that strong friend, or the person with the resources to help others. Sometimes we are the oak that shapes the ecosystem around us, that holds up, sustains, and shelters others. And the more we cultivate our own health, our material resources, and our body, the more often we are able to be that oak.

Certainly, this is not always possible. Also, there's a danger to being relied upon too often, because this can prevent people from doing the necessary work of providing for themselves. When we are in this role for too long, we can become defined by what we do and provide for others, rather than all the other things that we also are.

The Cups: The Path of Water and Emotions

The cups represent the cyclical path of developing our senses, our feeling, our imagination, and especially our connection to the world around us. Of course, this often also relates to love, but that love is not just the romantic sort.

The reason why these are all associated with water is because of the way that water flows in and out of all of life. The rain that falls from the sky was once water vapor rising from lakes, streams, oceans, and even our own sweat. When it falls, it joins the water on the earth as if it had never been apart from it, and it will do so again, and again, and again.

This is the same way our feelings and desires flow through the world. Beyond all our differences, we are composed of the very same things, and though our unique identities are certainly important, we are each like drops of rain rejoining the sea.

Desire is a flow between us, and love is another word for that flow. Sure, we also hate, and become angry, but these are just different currents in that same flow. And the cycle of the cups is there to teach us something profound about all these currents, and that larger flow itself.

Here are a few general questions you might find really helpful to ask yourself when cups cards show up in your readings:

- How is my heart right now?
- What desires connect me to others?
- How do I feel, and how do I feel about these feelings?
- How do I respond to other people's emotions, and are these responses really helpful for them? Are they really helpful for me?

Ace of Cups

Aces represent the beginning of a new cycle, an initiatory phase, the first steps in a process, and the Ace of Cups is the initial moment of letting feeling flow through us. It's a moment of opening, of release, the early excitement when something — or someone — has our attention.

The cups speak to the creative force that arises in us when we allow our passion, love, and our emotions to flow from us like water. The key point for this is "allow," which is an active choice. Like opening a faucet, that force and flow is only released through our conscious choices.

One of the words we have for this creative force is "love," but it's important to understand love in a deeper sense. Rather than just a strong emotion or a feeling of attachment for someone, love is a conscious choice to direct our attention toward the person or thing we *choose* to love. And the Ace of Cups speaks to this initial choice, and the great power which this opens up in us.

When this moment arises, we feel more engaged with the world around us. Passionate people seem to live life more fully than those who avoid strong emotions or who withdraw from the world, because they seem to feel everything — both joy and sorrow — more deeply.

The Ace of Cups is often drawn with multiple streams overflowing out of a filled chalice. The important thing to remember from this is that the flow is outward, not inward.

An easy mistake to make when interpreting this card is to focus on the subject of your passion, rather than on the awakening of that passion itself. Though there might be a new relationship or a new project that has your attention, the card is specifically speaking to the awakening of the feelings within you and your active choice to let them flow from you.

So, wherever this card appears in a reading, it might be helpful to ask what feelings seem to be welling up in you at the moment, and how you feel about those feelings. If they feel overwhelming to you, or if you've felt particularly "dry" or uninspired, it could be because you are trying to hold back too much, blocking these forces rather than letting them flow freely.

All aces are generally positive, even though they don't predict the outcome of something, just the beginning. In a past position, it may also be a call to deepen your passion and to seek larger channels for it.

Two of Cups

While the Ace of Cups speaks to the awakening of passion and the creative force of conscious love within us, the Two of Cups speaks to a mutual flow of this force between people.

This mutual flow and exchange can often occur in romantic relationships, and many traditional interpretations of this card focus heavily on this aspect. Unfortunately, looking only at this possibility obscures the deeper meaning of this card, and can even potentially mislead a person into feeling as if the card predicts such a relationship.

Instead, it's more helpful to think about the creative power that arises when we share our passion with another person. The excitement we feel when we find out someone else feels the same way we do leads us to feel more connected and more alive. Their passion increases our passion, and our passion increases theirs.

And though I just warned of the dangers of assuming this card refers to romantic relationships, sex is a good way of understanding the deeper meaning of this card. When two people become aroused by each other, their bodies respond by increasing the flow of blood and other fluids. This physical response is also what happens emotionally when we share our passions with each other. Our desire for life increases as theirs increases, and this is how new life — physically and metaphorically — is born into the world.

So, when this card appears, try to look first for the places in your life where you are currently sharing your passion with others, or where you might want to try doing so. This exchange can certainly refer to what occurs in an actual romantic relationship — whether new or more enduring. If you've been with someone for a long time, the Two of Cups could be suggesting a new exchange of passion may soon occur between you. If it doesn't refer to a romantic relationship, there's probably another kind of partnership available to you.

In a past position, it can sometimes refer to a pre-occupation with a former lover or a longing for the earlier passion of a current relationship. If the latter, remember that relationships — like all else in life — have cycles, and try to embrace this current part of the cycle.

Three of Cups

In the Ace of Cups, passion and love awaken in us and start to overflow. In the Two of Cups, it flows mutually between us and another. In the Three of Cups, it begins to flow out into the world.

This card is often illustrated with three figures — usually women — raising filled cups in celebration. Such acts of celebration are the basis of all friendships, an enjoyment and delight in the happiness of those we love. Rather than the competitive fear and scarcity mentality that tells us the success of one means the failure of another, the Three of Cups reminds us that joy and love expand the world around us.

The kind of celebration and friendship which this card represents is an increasingly rare sort in our societies, especially the older one gets. With the pressures of work or family and all the other demands of life, we have less and less time to be around friends or to celebrate the little things in life. And when we neglect these vital parts of our lives, we become isolated, worn down, and find the passion drain from our souls. We can then find ourselves trying to substitute what we are missing through sources that only perpetuate that isolation.

It's been said that the opposite of addiction is human connection, and this certainly is true. At the same time, it's essential for us not to see our friendships as a strategy for bettering our lives or increasing our happiness, but rather as something that exists for its own sake. Friendship needs no justification, and the sharing of mutual joy with others is a core aspect of being human.

When this card appears in a reading, it's pointing to this kind of expansive exchange between people. It's probably a great time to meet up with a friend or a few friends. Don't worry if you don't have a good pretext for doing so — but if you really need one, tell them the Tarot told you to. And if your friendships are often based on sharing struggles or talking through problems, try instead to just enjoy being with each other. Or, if you don't currently have many friendships, this card could be gently suggesting you seek more out.

In a past position, this card can be a good opportunity to reflect on the positive ways that friends have influenced who you are. In a future position, it can also suggest an upcoming celebration or the need for one.

Four of Cups

Fours represent structure, and cups represent the flow of passion and feelings. So, taking these two aspects together, there seems to be a deep contradiction or paradox in this card. After all, how do you structure passion?

The key to understanding the Four of Cups is remembering that the other fours refer not just to structure, but also to restructuring and rest. If you think of the numbers as climbing stairs, the four is a short landing before you climb the rest of them.

So, the Four of Cups refers to a kind of pause in the expansion of our passions and desires where we begin to see both their power and their limits. Sometimes, we need to withdraw from intense feelings so that we can understand them better.

We also learn in such moments that we can channel our passions. Without developing these skills, very strong emotions — such as anger — can overwhelm us and cause destruction in our lives. Even "positive" emotions such as joy can be overdone: in traditional Chinese medicine, too much joy and excitement are understood as dangerous for the heart.

If you drink alcohol, consider how the warm feeling of a few drinks can turn into the irritated and out-of-control feeling of too many. Or how an enjoyment of a dessert can turn into the discomfort of having over-indulged. Or how any pleasure or passion can lose its delight when we take it to excess. Certainly, there are times we need to let what we feel flow out of us. But there are also important moments when we need to hold back, to reserve some part of ourselves, or even to say "no" to a potentially enjoyable thing.

The appearance of the Four of Cups in a reading may be speaking to such moments of excess, or of the need to withdraw from intense passions for a little while. If so, try not to feel as if you're somehow being punished or are denying yourself a pleasure. Instead, think of it as a gentle reminder that you are ultimately the only one responsible for channeling your passion.

It could also be referring to the feeling of being bored in life. This is not something to fear. Think of such moments as a rest for your heart before new passions arrive.

Also, if in a past position, it may be time to rejoin life again and either seek out new passions or cultivate previous ones.

Five of Cups

Every five is a crisis point where the increasing development in the previous four cards is complicated and then transformed. These are rarely pleasant moments, but they always result in powerful truths.

In most depictions of the Five of Cups, a grieving figure mourns three overturned cups while ignoring the two cups still filled behind him. Often, a distant bridge over a river is shown, possibly leading the figure back home.

Grief, sorrow, and disappointment are all incredibly difficult emotions to work through, especially because they are each rooted in the equally strong emotions of love, joy, and hope. The more deeply we loved someone, the more joy we felt from a thing, and the more hope we put into a possibility, the deeper our feelings of loss become.

In such times, we struggle to see what else still exists and what will come next. And, if we remain too long in such moments, we can become stuck in them, lose our way, and fall into depression and despair.

The Five of Cups is about the necessity of fully feeling through these moments of loss. We must go through them with our heart open to the pain, because this is the only way to heal. Closing ourselves off from this process can make us physically sick and emotionally stunted, leading us to become bitter, cold, and afraid to hope and love again.

Part of this process is turning back "home," back to our hearts, the core of who we are, and also to the places and people into which our passions still flow. It can be quite difficult to see those things in our darkest moments, but they are still there with us, regardless.

In a present position, this card can be speaking to such a moment of disappointment or grief. If so, let yourself feel your way through the loss, and be kind to yourself throughout this. Also, in a present or a past position, it can be referring to an unhealed disappointment that is leading you either to feel depressed or like you are a "victim." You may need to do some extra work to move past such a situation.

In future positions, this card can be cautioning you against putting too much hope in something, especially if you have a habit of projecting your hopes onto other people or future prospects. It may be healthier to focus on what is before you, and to make your current situation better.

Six of Cups

The Six of Cups is traditionally associated with memory and innocence. To understand why, keep in mind that sixes represent the integration of the crises in the fives. In the Five of Cups, we begin to understand how grief and disappointment can drain the joy out of life and lead us to fear becoming attached or hopeful. In the Six of Cups, we finally remember there are two unspilled cups, and that even more can be filled.

Another way of thinking of this card is that it is a return to the home of our heart, and all those that have shared that home with us. The memories of past loves, of warm moments of family, or of playful banter with friends all shape who we are and what we find most important in life.

Certainly, we all have some less-than-happy memories, but this card isn't about them at all. In fact, the Six of Cups tells us something about memory itself. We are always "teaching each other how to love," and the choice to remember the best of these lessons is how we let love continue to shape our world. Rather than becoming defined by loss, the Six of Cups tells us that we can instead define ourselves by love.

A helpful practice to connect to these moments is to envision the younger versions of yourself in these memories. Try to picture the giddy first moments of the times you've fallen in love, try to feel the warm sunlight and salt breeze of a happy day at the beach, the contented feeling after your favorite birthday party. And then, remind yourself — because it's true — that these are not just memories, but also ways of being in the world that are always available to you.

In any position of a reading, as with all sixes, this card is quite positive. In a past position, it's a really great time to indulge in the richness of your happiest memories: let them wrap around you like a warm bear hug. This applies for a present and future position, as well.

Also in a present position, you may want to try reconnecting with a long-lost friend or a favorite family member you haven't spoken to for a while. Also, try to approach the current moment with a childlike innocence. Enjoy simple pleasures and quiet loves, realizing that we are always creating future memories.

In a future position, you may also want to consider planning some time to gather family and friends together, or making an extra effort to show up to such a gathering.

Seven of Cups

The unsettling and liberating message of the Seven of Cups is that we have both the power and the responsibility to decide *what* we desire, and also *what we do* with that desire.

Our desires are not always our own. Certainly, we know this on an intellectual level. Advertising wouldn't exist if it didn't work, and as much as we pretend that we buy the kinds of things that we do out of our own free will, we know this isn't really true.

This is just as true when it comes to standards of beauty. Especially because of social media representations, we can find ourselves lost in endless self-criticism and comparison, compulsively chasing after well-crafted illusions which have very little basis in reality. Even our social and political allegiances, especially how we feel about people "not like us," are shaped by what others want us to feel and think.

Sometimes, we can mistake symbols and objects for the things they represent to us, and thus get caught in cycles of disillusionment. Sometimes, we project our hopes and goals onto others, or assume they are happier and more satisfied in life than we are. And sometimes, the "fear of missing out" can prevent us from seeing the beautiful things already in our lives.

If you are currently struggling with knowing what you really want, you may find it helpful to ask yourself the same question twice. For instance, "what do I want?" And then, "what do I *really* want?" Sometimes, the answer is the same. Often, though, the second answer is the correct one. Or, if you are currently feeling unsatisfied about a situation, ask yourself whether the standards you are judging life by are really your own, and then ask yourself a second time.

Sometimes, the appearance of this card can be a challenge to deepen your commitment to your passions and desires, especially if you've become distracted by fears of "missing out" on other experiences, or you've become too focused on other potentials. In a past position, it could even point out how a current situation is the result of previous self-deception or being led too easily by impulses.

In a future position, it's especially important to beware of self-delusion or of projecting your hopes on others.

Eight of Cups

After the challenge of the Seven of Cups — in which we are asked what it is that we truly want — the Eight of Cups arrives and shows us how to truly find it.

Sometimes, dissatisfaction comes from being ungrateful for what we have. But it can also be a profound awareness that what we truly desire cannot be provided by our current circumstances, our social environment, or our mode of living. The Eight of Cups is about this second kind of dissatisfaction, and the deep transformation our hearts go through when we realize that what we want most isn't available to us.

Over a decade ago, this card kept appearing in every one of my readings, no matter how many times I shuffled. Back then, I was living in the United States, struggling to make ends meet in a city that no longer felt like home. That's why the card kept appearing: I was unsatisfied with my life, and I kept putting off following my heart's desire to move to Europe. And once I finally made that decision, the card stopped appearing.

Most traditional interpretations of this card are quite negative, but they miss the point. It can certainly sometimes refer to the moment when we realize a relationship is no longer reciprocal, or the need to "move on" from a situation that no longer feeds your soul. But these are only some of the potential meanings, and it's not helpful to focus on them.

I find that the best advice for this card's appearance is to focus on the moon hanging in the sky, and the unseen destination to which the figure in the card is traveling. The Eight of Cups is calling you to a deeper commitment to your own heart, urging you to seek what you truly desire.

This can sometimes take the form of a spiritual journey, or even a physical one to places that have profound meaning to you. Or, it can manifest as a temporary withdrawal from the world and the demands of others. Whatever form it takes, the purpose is to reconnect to what you most desire, and to then take the first steps to find it.

In a past position, it could suggest you're still struggling with a previous decision to move on from something, perhaps doubting if you made the correct choice. In a present position, it could be prompting you to look at the reasons for unhappiness in your life. And in a future position, it could be suggesting you need to expand what you think is emotionally possible in your life, and to recommit to your dreams.

Nine of Cups

The Nine of Cups is traditionally interpreted as quite positive, but with a subtle yet important caveat. And that's also how I think you should interpret it, too.

First of all, it's absolutely about the realization of your dreams, the fulfillment of your goals, and all the happiness that flows through you in such times. When it appears, especially in future positions, it indicates a time of celebration and the attainment of your wishes. The thing you desired has arrived, and you can now fully enjoy yourself.

But there is a mystery in every nine, a final challenge or obstacle in the cycle before its completion. In the Nine of Wands, we see a refined will struggling not to be defined by its struggles. In the Nine of Swords, a highly developed mind is challenged by the impossibility of perfection. In the Nine of Pentacles, we see material wealth and great health as merely a foundation, not the goal itself. And here, in the Nine of Cups, we see that even getting what we truly want is not the actual end goal of our desires.

To understand this, remember the traditional illustration of the Ace of Cups as a chalice overflowing. Like water, desire and love are forces that flow through us and back into us, and it's the flow itself that makes them what they are. Desire and love are movement, attraction, a kind of gravitational pull holding everything we are together and putting us in orbit around everything else in the world.

So, you may have gotten what you always wanted, or are about to. Congratulations! Really, you should celebrate and enjoy it. And if something still feels missing, or if it's not exactly what you hoped it would be, don't let that cast a shadow over it. Instead, remember that there will be even more things to desire, and that it's the desiring itself which is what makes us who we are.

Especially in a past position, you might be thinking, "what now?" Or, you might have trouble feeling fully grateful for what you've received or attained. In a present position, it's especially important to let yourself fully enjoy the life and love around you, even if others don't feel like celebrating, or even if some seem to harbor some resentment for your happiness. And in a future position, the positive aspects of this card are especially strong. You'll get your wish. Just be sure to recognize it when it arrives.

Ten of Cups

The true challenge of the Nine of Cups is to understand that the objects of your desire are not the goal of desire itself. In the Ten of Cups, we then see the kind of life and love we can experience when we've finally understood this.

Happiness is not a destination. Instead, it's a state of being that has been available to us all along. Like love, it's an active decision and a moment of surrender. We choose to let love flow through us, and we choose to let happiness into our lives.

Notice the word I used in that last sentence, "let." Another word we could use is "allow," or even "give ourselves permission." All these ways of describing the process are really about just opening ourselves up to something, rather than putting up barriers and obstacles to keep it out.

That's the core meaning of the Ten of Cups, and the completion of the cycle of this suit. We are constantly chasing after happiness and contentment, and that endless pursuit is crucial to our lives as humans. However, the chase can only ever result in the recognition that happiness and contentment are never actually outside of us.

Traditionally, the Ten of Cups is thought to refer to marriage, and though this can sometimes be the case, it's helpful to think of how marriage is seen in traditional societies. In those societies, finding a life partner meant the completion of one cycle of love (the search for a partner) which then manifests in the beginning of a new cycle of love (the nurture and care of family).

The appearance of this card is always deeply positive, no matter its position. It points both to the attainment of what we desire and also a moment of understanding that desire in a new and more complete way.

In a future position, you can certainly expect a time of great happiness to arrive, especially if you do the work now of dismantling any remaining barriers to it. In a present position, it's probably already here, or lingering just outside, waiting for you to invite it in. And in a past position, this card may be inviting you to look at previous moments of joy not as a past that is gone forever, but rather as a home you can return to at any time, including right now.

Page of Cups

A good way to understand the Page of Cups is to picture a child hosting a tea party with stuffed animals or other toys. Despite being "imaginary," each guest is treated as a fully-developed person, and the child responds to each in precisely the ways that we would hope to respond to actual people.

This play-acting points to something innate about human empathy. We are able to understand and often predict how others might feel about something by using our imagination, and that imagination is a crucial tool to also understanding ourselves.

The Page of Cups is essentially about this power and the knowledge it brings to us. Like all other pages, it represents an initial "innocent" approach, unburdened — but also uninformed — by more complex ways of being. It's a playful approach to emotions and feelings, the early moments of joy, and the whimsical delight of a new sensation before it develops into a deeper passion.

Like all court cards, we pass through the ways of being represented by the Page of Cups many, many times in our lives. We can always find delight in the world, no matter how hard life might get. We can always find new feelings, new delights, and new loves. The playful, giggling laughter of old women sitting around a card table sounds just like the laughter you'd expect to hear from young girls, because that laughter is always available to us. We just sometimes need to forget everything else we've seen in life to remember it again.

When the Page of Cups appears, it's quite often a call to "feel" again, especially if you've recently withdrawn from emotions. When we close ourselves off — sometimes a very necessary act — we can forget to open ourselves back up again, and this can lead us to become uninspired or become numb. Fortunately, all that's really needed to get back to such states is a sense of play and wonder. Perhaps set some time aside to daydream, and see what comes your way.

Occasionally, the Page of Cups can also be a suggestion not to remain too long on the surface level of feelings — yours or others. By taking too light of an approach to emotions, we can sometimes hurt others or miss really powerful states of being that seem initially too complex or out of reach to us.

Knight of Cups

In the Arthurian myth of the Fisher King, a young knight searching for a powerful magical item — the grail — arrives at the castle of a wounded king. All the lands this king rules have become barren, as if under a dark spell. To set everything right again, to heal the king and also to obtain the grail, all the young knight needs to do is to ask an obvious question.

In most stories, the knight doesn't ask the question, because he is either too shy or he is trying to be too polite. But in versions where he does, he shows us precisely what the Knight of Cups is trying to tell us.

There is always some risk in desire, especially in romantic desire. It takes a lot of courage to ask someone out on a first date, because they might say "no." But when we really look at our fear, we might also find we're just as much afraid of a potential "yes."

The same goes for other hopes, desires, and dreams. It can feel safer to stay in the realm of unfulfilled possibility, imagining what "might be" rather than daring to find out what "can be."

The Knight of Cups asks the question and takes that risk. It's a card full of daring and asking and letting yourself be vulnerable, despite the fact that you'll have no assurance your wish will manifest. You might fall flat on your face, experience rejection, humiliation, maybe even despair. But you'll also never know unless you ask.

Sure, this is not always the best approach to take in life, and our society can be quite harsh to romantic dreamers. Yet at the same time, there would be no romance films without them. In other words, we both chide them and celebrate them.

If the Knight of Cups has appeared in your reading and if you are struggling with indecision in matters of the heart, it might be time to ask that question or take a risk. There's no guarantee it will go well, but there's also no guarantee that it won't, either. Ask yourself if you'd really rather not know what more is possible. And if that sounds an awful fate, go find out.

Its appearance could also relate to an inner transformation of your desires or emotions. You may be in a point where your feelings about someone or something are deepening, and it could be time to acknowledge this to yourself. Or, maybe your initial flirtation (with a person or a dream) now requires a commitment, and you could benefit from some time really exploring your feelings about the matter — and their consequences.

Queen of Cups

Imagine the kind of emotional security and certainty you would need to feel free to love and to be loved without getting tripped up by your own self-conscious doubts and fears.

You don't actually have to imagine this, because it's always available to you. And that's what the Queen of Cups is here to remind you.

In the Major Arcana, The Star signifies a deep connection to the sources of inspiration that flow through us. The Queen of Cups says something similar, except the connection and flow in this card is between our own hearts and the hearts of others.

One of the classic associations of this card is with acting, and this is a really useful way of understanding it. The best actors are able not just to convince us that they are someone else, but they are also able to make us feel what their character is feeling. And then, when the play or the film is over, those actors then return to who they really are, without ever losing sight of their true nature.

This is the kind of being in the world that the Queen of Cups describes. We can move through life, encountering and even taking on the emotions of others, and then also still remain ourselves. Much like putting on a costume or a fancy outfit, we can be many things and feel many ways and yet always keep in touch with our core being.

Appearing in a reading, the Queen of Cups often calls you to this kind of confident flow. Especially if you've been unsure of yourself or your intuitions about a situation, maybe you need to put your doubts aside for a while. Try on a new trust or a new attitude towards things in the same way you might try on a new outfit. See how it makes you feel, if it fits well, and what kind of confidence it brings to you.

Also, if you are often afraid of becoming overwhelmed by your own emotions or those of others, this card could be pointing you toward a new way of experiencing them. Perhaps imagine them as waves in the sea, passing through the ocean without affecting what is deep underneath.

On the other hand, if you are very often caught up in the emotions of others or your own, the Queen of Cups' appearance could be a suggestion that you have been too long in this state and your heart is getting waterlogged. In such cases, try to dry out a bit before delving into the emotional world again.

King of Cups

The King of Cups is the state of being we reach when what we want is also what is available to us. At such points in our life, nothing seems to be able to shake us, and even the simplest things can make us feel happy, satisfied, and content.

Often, satisfaction and contentment are thought of as negative states. When someone goes out of their way to win an argument, the loser might throw up their hands and ask, "are you satisfied now?" Or, a person longing for more in their life might be told by others, "you should learn to be content with what you have." But to get a more positive understanding, consider the warm full feeling after a really good meal with friends or family. Also, imagine the feeling in your belly after a really deep, long laugh. They're both the same feeling, and that's the full-heartedness the King of Cups represents.

The key to this state is being fully present in your life, and this is why the King of Cups is also associated with emotional "maturity." When we understand that we can direct our emotions, rather than letting them direct us, we are able to decide which of them we will cultivate and which of them will set aside for other times. So, in a moment where we can enjoy ourselves fully, we choose to do so, rather than letting other emotions get in the way.

This kind of maturity doesn't mean we classify some emotions as bad and others as good, or that we put tight controls on our heart. Instead, we make space for each of them. This means that we then also need to fully experience these other feelings when the time is right for them.

The King of Cups often appears in readings when there's a need to either direct our emotions in a more conscious way, or to let ourselves experience the present moment more fully. Both are essentially the same thing, and one way of looking at this is to remember the association of cups and emotions with water, and then imagine that you are opening and closing floodgates or locks on a canal. Let some feelings fill you while others wait for another time.

There is of course a negative aspect here, as with all other court cards. Sometimes, we can try to control our emotional states too much, especially if we are privileging the easier ones over the more difficult. In such cases, we can wear ourselves out, become estranged from deeper feelings, or even find repressed feelings breaking the dams we built against them.

The Swords: The Path of Air and Mind

Communication, the intellect, and the mind are represented by the suit of swords in Tarot, and this immediately tends to give the sense that there's a constant theme of conflict within many of the cards.

In fact, this association is at least half-true. Ideals and beliefs clash, and suddenly there is religious, civil, and political strife. And if you look at most conflicts between people, or between nations, they certainly seem to start as wars of words.

But words are also able to prevent strife, to stop wars, and unite peoples. Ideas and inventions that benefit everyone are just as common — if not more so — than those that bring harm.

That's not just the power of the mind, but also of air. "Inspiration" comes from the Latin word for breath, and the word "aspire," which basically means "longing" and "reaching for," comes from the same root. Like water, air connects us to each other — for better, and for worse.

The cards in the suit speak to the development of our mind and our ability to communicate what is within us. Sure, there is conflict, but there is also so much else as well.

These questions may help you when thinking about what the swords cards in your readings are speaking to:

- What do I *really* think?
- How do I express myself, and what do I do when others misunderstand?
- Which ideas are most important to me, and which ones are only casual opinions?
- How is the way I see the world shaped by what others think?
- Do I see my mind and my thoughts as an enemy? And if so, how can I change this?

Ace of Swords

Aces always indicate a new beginning or an "initiation," and the Ace of Swords speaks directly to the birth of something new in the mind or intellectual sphere.

If you've felt a bit bored with your life — losing interest in the familiar things that once sustained you, or finding yourself constantly looking for distraction through social media or entertainment — the Ace of Swords is a great card to receive. It suggests that some new idea or new perspective has arrived that will whet your mental appetite for more knowledge.

There's a particular mental passivity our societies actively encourage. While there's nothing inherently wrong with being entertained, much of what we enjoy is essentially fed to us. Even the work of learning about a subject that interests us is now mostly automated through search engine suggestions. It's all made quite easy, but much like the effect of regularly eating highly-processed, sugar-rich foods, our minds start to become addicted to immediate rushes that can never sustain us.

The Ace of Swords reminds that you have control over your mental attention, and you can direct your mind and its thoughts. In fact, you have a profound responsibility to yourself to do just that, and you're at a place where any such effort will feel quite thrilling for you. This is just as applicable if you're considering a new field of study or trying to find a way to communicate your ideas as it is if you've been struggling with boredom or patterns of unhelpful and even destructive thoughts. Also, if you've struggled with focusing your attention on things important to you, you may find this a great time to tackle those tasks.

Likewise, if there's been some confusion in your life, or if you've had difficulty expressing your thoughts about a matter, the Ace of Swords may be pointing the way to finding the clarity you need.

In future positions, this card could be suggesting you seek out the clarity it represents, or that the work implied in the other cards will result in that clarity. In a past position, it might be inviting you to re-examine your initial thoughts, reasoning, or plans to check if you're still on that path, or if you've perhaps become distracted somehow.

Two of Swords

The traditional illustration of the Two of Swords can be a bit unsettling. The crossed blades and the blindfold seem to denote confusion and also fear, and some interpretations of this card play up a sense of dread and indecision. But the moon typically depicted in the sky behind the figure points to a deeply liberating truth.

Your brain isn't a sense organ, and it cannot feel. Instead, its role is to sort through all the actual sensations the body experiences, to interpret them, and to then make decisions based upon that information. And, as The Moon shows us, misinterpretation is quite easy to do.

One of the most effective ways of understanding the relationship between our body and our thoughts is through meditation. By learning how our mind misinterprets bodily sensations (often resulting in anxiety), we can then hone our intellect and make better decisions about our life.

You may be at a point where you need to make a decision, and you are struggling with your feelings about your options. Or maybe you don't even know how you feel yet, and are worried that thinking too deeply about the matter will bring up some disruptive and unpleasant feelings. It's also possible that an opinion you hold has been challenged, and you're not yet sure how you had come to that original conclusion.

Remember that the twos are cards of change and are the first part of the transformation journey the ace initiates. Like the creative tension of the Two of Pentacles, the Two of Swords is an intellectual tension that can sharpen your mind. This decision point and the self-knowledge it invites of you is a crucial step to the development of your mind and your expression, so do not fear it.

In all positions, the appearance of this card suggests a need to examine the relationship between your reasoning and your feelings about a situation. Ask yourself if you're accurately understanding your senses about a matter. In a past position, it could be asking you to revisit a previous decision or to look at a memory in a new light. If it appears in a future position, it could also indicate the need to settle your mind, understand your motives, and weigh all options in a situation before deciding.

Three of Swords

The Three of Swords is often called the "heartbreak" card, and receiving it in a reading — especially in a future position — can often make you feel like your heart is about to stop. But the cups deal with emotions and love, not the swords. That means this card, even with those three blades piercing the heart, is trying to tell us something else.

There are many times we avoid speaking our mind out of fear. We might worry about the pain it might cause another, or we might fear others will not like us because of what we say. We may even avoid situations (including relationships) or promising opportunities because we're afraid we might get emotionally hurt.

The Three of Swords is a reminder that pain, grief, sorrow, — and yes, heartbreak — are inevitable. They'll come, no matter how hard we try to avoid them. And since they are inevitable, there's absolutely no use to any of our mental strategies designed to prevent them.

This doesn't mean that life is itself a tragedy or that we should be defined by our sorrows. On the contrary: it's exactly those moments of pain that make the rest of life sweeter and more full of joy. And in those moments when our heart seems to be breaking and we are so sad that we cannot eat, our mind can remind us of this larger perspective.

The appearance of this card is always a call to look directly at how the fear of hurt, pain, and loss have defined our thoughts. It's also a gentle invitation to change any defense mechanisms and avoidance strategies we have developed. Have we closed off our horizons and shut out the world because of our past sorrows? Have we become defined by hurtful words or experiences and now find it hard to see ourselves or others clearly?

In past positions, it may be urging you to look at the way a sorrow — maybe a previous relationship, a sense of failure, or a traumatic event — is still shaping your thoughts and behavior. In a present position, if you are currently experiencing grief, this card is reminding you not to shape your thinking by it. And in a future position, contemplate the inevitability of loss, and ask yourself if your fear of getting hurt is really worth closing yourself off from deep connection.

Four of Swords

While writing this guide, a person very close to me experienced a horrible work burnout. As happens quite often with intellectual professionals, he'd failed to take conscious time off, and instead tried to think his way through the exhaustion, stress, and anxiety he felt.

The Four of Swords is the key to not getting into such positions. Fours are structure, and this card's message is that we must structure our thoughts and mental activity, giving ourselves both time to think and also time not to think.

Structuring our mental lives is an especially difficult practice in modern life, especially because we often fill moments of silence with noise and our downtime with media distractions. This means we are "always on," without any real rest or silence to rejuvenate ourselves. Being constantly in this state can mean we're not aware of which thoughts are our own and which ones have been fed to us. Also, it can mean we don't always realize how exhausted this makes us until it causes a crisis.

The Four of Swords reminds you that structure is not only possible but also essential to thinking clearly. Becoming conscious of how much time we spend in distraction (such as using a "screen time" tracker on devices) and then making intentional decisions to change this can be quite powerful. Also, using time-tested ways of organizing your thoughts (journaling, for example) can help relieve some of the mental pressure of keeping track of too many things.

Structuring your non-thinking time is just as crucial. Even if you cannot afford a week-end retreat or a vacation, taking a day away from all digital communication — like leaving your phone at home and going for a very long walk — can help you get out of your head and give your mind a rest. Even if you don't think of yourself as an intellectual, you will absolutely benefit from some time intentionally set aside to not think.

In a past position, the Four of Swords may also refer to a period of recent illness, fatigue, or depression that is now ending. If so, see if there was a connection between overthinking and that bodily response. In a present or future position, it's time to carve out some time for yourself, organize your thoughts, and give yourself some space to just be.

Five of Swords

In the Five of Swords, a battle has just finished, and those defeated walk away in humiliation. Fives are the crises inherent in the relationship between an aspect of ourselves and others, and this card points to the crises of arguments and mental conflicts.

Most of us have experienced the moment when differences of opinion or arguments suddenly separate us from people close to us. Especially when it comes to politics or to social issues, we can find that strongly held beliefs can cut through even the closest friendships, and we worry nothing can repair the damage.

Sometimes, we can care so much about being right that we forget the humanity of those we argue with. Especially if our belief systems divide the world between "good" and "evil," we can find ourselves demonizing those who believe differently. Also, in arguments between friends or lovers, we can even be quite cruel, using insults we know will hurt them deeply.

In any such conflict, it's important to examine our own beliefs and conclusions, and to trace the ways our ideas shape how we see ourselves and others. There's always a risk of becoming too identified with our opinions on a matter, our ideological or political allegiances, or even with our personal tastes. And sometimes, the opinions we hold aren't even our own, but have been shaped by our environments or by media.

Conflict is inevitable, and having differences of opinion is what makes the world richer. Arguments sharpen our minds, giving us an opportunity to test our ideas against others. But winning an argument can sometimes feel as costly as losing. We must be clear on what's truly important to us.

If you've recently felt hurt by a conflict, don't let the experience make you feel bitter. Also, this card could be suggesting that it's time to reconcile with someone, especially if it appears in a past position. In a future position, this card may be warning that a situation is heading towards such a conflict. This isn't bad, but be clear in your thinking about it now.

In all positions, remember that you are not your beliefs or opinions, and the same is true for others. It's possible there could be a false image of someone causing you to react negatively to them, or others might be responding to their own misconceptions about you. Communicate as clearly as possible, and try to cut through any confusion with patience and grace.

Six of Swords

This card is often associated with transitions and intentional, long journeys, which are in some ways the same thing. When we make long journeys, we learn more about who we are and what we believe, and at the end we often find ourselves significantly changed. Transitions — whether relocations, changes in careers, the birth of a child, marriage, the death of a family member, or physical changes like puberty or menopause — likewise shift our perspectives and show us something different about life we could not have understood previously.

There is a profound calm portrayed in many illustrations of this card, with the figure guiding the boat doing so with a relaxed stance. The waters over which the boat glides are untroubled: the journeys and transitions this card points to are not emotionally unsettling.

In the previous card, we begin to see the role of the mind in conflict. We get a sense of how our opinions shape the way we see ourselves and others, and we begin to understand the limitations of our thoughts. The Six of Swords is the integration of that knowledge, a deepening of our beliefs, and especially the development of a neutral stance in relationship to ideas and belief systems.

When we have our beliefs shaken up or our perspectives challenged, our initial reaction can be to cling tighter to them, to dig in our heels and become defensive. The Six of Swords is what happens when we instead look at our viewpoints and those of others without emotional attachment or prejudice. We remember that we will change our mind again and again throughout our lives, and we learn not to take our ways of thinking too seriously.

As with all sixes, this card is always quite positive in a reading. It's pointing to a moment of resolution and reflection, like a passenger gazing calmly at the passing landscape on a long train ride. If you're in a moment of transition right now and are uncertain of the future, trust that the place you're going will make more sense when you get there.

Very often in present and future positions, it's a call to take a journey, or to seek out other ways to experience life differently. In past positions, it may also be reminding you to notice how you once felt differently about a current matter, or how current thoughts are rooted in a previous way of thinking that no longer applies.

Seven of Swords

In myth, folklore, and even everyday speech, foxes have a reputation for being cunning. Cunning originally just meant "knowing" or "skilled," but it's also had an extra sense of a dangerous or unpredictable knowledge that can be used both to deceive and also to see through deception.

The Seven of Swords is all about this kind of knowledge. Sevens represent the entrance of an external or unknown influence into a situation. In this card, it can be an unforeseen complication, a hidden motive, or a stroke of genius which transforms a situation.

Negative interpretations of this card tend to focus heavily on the figure of the thief as a sign something is being taken from you. This way of looking at the card may sometimes be helpful in guiding you to become more aware of dishonest people, but I've found this to be quite rare.

Instead, it's more helpful to look at what the thief has just accomplished. Stealing weapons from an armed military camp is quite a clever feat, and it's quite possible the thief has prevented the deaths of others by doing so. Regardless of the outcome, though, the thief has certainly done something unexpected, and the soldiers didn't notice his actions.

The Seven of Swords might be drawing your attention to an aspect you haven't noticed about a situation or a problem. Maybe there's some hidden influence or deeper concern guiding your actions or those of others. Or maybe you need to try a completely different way of approaching a matter.

This card also points to the relationship between the intellect and intuition, especially if The Moon or cups cards show up in the same reading. When we let our intuition inform our intellect, an unsolvable problem can suddenly seem quite easy.

Be careful of relying only on cunning, though. Especially if you tend to rely on half-truths or minor deceptions to avoid conflict, these can accumulate so much that they trap you. If this card is in a past position, it may be speaking to this problem and challenging you to be more honest.

In present positions, give extra attention to details. Is there something you've missed that is making a situation more difficult than it needs to be? Or, do you need to gather more knowledge before making a decision? The same also applies in future positions, with the additional possibility that some new factor will arrive that you cannot predict yet, so it might be a good idea to hold off on a decision until then.

Eight of Swords

Despite the apparent negative imagery of this card, the Eight of Swords is actually quite positive. To understand this, compare it to the other eights: the accelerated "cosmic" energy in the Eight of Wands, the sense of purpose and diligence in the Eight of Pentacles, and the expansion of desire in the Eight of Cups.

In the Eight of Swords, we see the blindfold of the Two of Swords again, but this time the woman is also bound. She has most likely done this to herself. And though the swords around her seem to form a wall, she has walked through them.

The Eight of Swords represents the stage in mental development where we discover how patterns of thinking — underlying structures — shape how we think and what kind of information we get from the world.

Many forms of therapy work by helping a person look at the patterns of thinking which lead them to become trapped in self-destructive situations. They don't stop there, though. Instead, they help the person learn to change their way of thinking, to create new patterns, and to reshape their lives according to more helpful ways of seeing themselves and the world.

The Eight of Swords speaks to this same process. It's the moment when we realize the limitations we've imposed on ourselves, and finally learn to break free of mental prisons whose doors were never locked.

When this card appears in a reading, it's very likely pointing to some way that you have limited yourself. Certainly, these limits might have first come from external sources (unkind words, traumatic relationships, moments of failure or shame), but you hold the ultimate responsibility here. And as with the other eights, any effort you put in now will be particularly powerful.

In a past or present position, ask yourself whether or not a situation you are facing has been caused by self-imposed mental limits or unhelpful beliefs. Don't fear this self-analysis — you're about to learn something that can liberate you.

In a future position, this card might suggest you wait on making judgments, coming to conclusions, responding, or reacting to a situation. You might not have all the information you need yet, or you might not be in the best position to understand everything. If this feels hard, contemplate the wisdom of The Hanged Man.

Nine of Swords

Perfectionism is a self-defeating fear that can often prevent us from acting in the world. By trying to make things perfect, we are really attempting to avoid the potential for criticism. But nothing can ever truly be perfect, and we are very often our most brutal and vicious critics.

This fear of criticism and failure is actually a fear of social isolation. We want others to think well of us, and even the most fiercely independent people still want to be loved.

Remember the difficult message of the Three of Swords? In that card, we learn to see how the strategies and defense mechanisms we develop to avoid sorrow and pain are completely useless. Mental maturity requires that we accept the inevitability of loss and heartbreak, instead of fearing it so much we avoid life and experiences.

The Nine of Swords speaks a similar truth, except that the inevitabilities we are now called to accept are isolation, loneliness, and the potential for failure. No matter how hard we try, we will never be able to control how others see us. There will always be times when others do not understand or accept our ideas, reasons, or choices, and we will often need to make decisions that can lead to separation and disconnection.

Refusing to accept this truth causes quite a lot of damage. It can lead us to diminish ourselves or to manipulate others, to become deceptive, paranoid, or depressed. It can completely drain the life out of us, separate us from sources of inspiration, and lead us to procrastinate endlessly. Or, just as likely, it can make us pessimistic about the world and ourselves.

This all can feel quite hard, especially if you are currently struggling with loneliness, depression, or a sense of failure. In a future position, this card can feel particularly frightening, but if you let it scare you than you're not understanding its lesson. The Nine of Swords shows that the path out of despair is acceptance, rather than indulging our darkest thoughts and fears.

In other positions, you may find it quite helpful to look into places your fears have cut you off — or are currently cutting you off — from others or from your goals. Thank these fears for their help, but let them know they are no longer needed.

In rarer instances, this card can also point to a feeling of guilt. It may be time for an apology or other ways of making amends.

Ten of Swords

Artists all know the moment when a piece of art is complete, and yet it doesn't really feel like it. The end of a novel is often the hardest bit to write, the last touches of paint on a canvas can feel the most uncertain. And even when we are finally able to declare it done, the act of letting it go completely can feel like something has been ripped out from inside of us.

Traditional interpretations of this card will tell you it's about betrayal or the experience of a painful ending. But these are only some of the potential results of the transformation this card represents. Instead, it's most helpful to focus on that internal struggle we feel when something we've worked so hard on — or invested so much of our time into — is now finished.

This can apply to massive worldview shifts, such as when we no longer believe the core tenets of a religion or political ideology. Or, it can refer to the end of a career, relationship, or intellectual project — whether or not we are the ones initiating its ending. It can also apply to social standing, reputation, or identity, especially if we are realizing we need to define ourselves to others in a wholly new way.

The Ten of Swords echoes the same tension of the Ten of Wands. That card speaks to the moment we need to let go of the responsibilities we have taken on because none of it is necessary any longer. The challenge of this card is letting go of all the mental effort we've poured into something and moving on to something else.

A metaphor which might help is this. Imagine the difficult transition of a soldier returning home from war, having seen both horror and heroism. "Regular" life can initially make no sense to such a person, and it can be hard to let go of the sense of immediacy that war demands. The key is transforming that urgency into *presence*, existing fully in life even when there is no imminent danger.

If this card is referring to a major change in your life or way of thinking, try to look at what is happening as the beginnings of a rebirth, and read the interpretation of Death if you need some extra help. Or, if you're a student, an artist, or someone else who works often with their mind or expression, maybe it's time to declare something complete. In a past position, this card could also be reminding you not to fall back on old ways of thinking, and in a future position, a chance to redefine yourself may be on its way.

Page of Swords

To connect to the meaning of this card, imagine a young child tracing fingers over the words of a college-level science textbook and staring with a detached curiosity at the graphs and diagrams on the page. The child doesn't actually understand anything in the textbook, yet if you were to look at this child's face, you'd see a surprising seriousness, revealing inexpressible thoughts.

That's the kind of mental approach that the Page of Swords describes, and it's more positive that it might seem at first glance. In fact, it's the kind of approach we need to take whenever we encounter complicated problems or tasks that require skills or experience that we don't have yet.

Again, think of the child with the textbook. The child doesn't yet know there are different levels of reading and that it will take many years to understand the kind of writing in that book. Much like the innocence of The Fool, the Page of Swords doesn't know how complicated things might be, and that "ignorance" actually helps us start the journey towards knowledge and wisdom.

When this card appears, it can be calling you to take this kind of mental approach to a problem. There are things you don't know yet, and that's okay. Rather than trying to understand everything at once, approach each part with curiosity, and try not to let your preconceived notions of a situation get in the way.

It could also be gently pointing out that you've remained too long in such a state, and it's time to go deeper. This can happen to us when we take too much of a superficial or detached approach to problems, or if we've come to rely too much on other people telling us how a thing really is.

In both aspects, what you are really being called to is the development of your mind and intellectual capacities. Such a development starts first with a curiosity about the world and about new ways of understanding it. Let that curiosity guide you in these first steps. That's what it does best.

Swords are not just thought, but also communication. This card might also be suggesting you try expressing yourself in a new way.

Knight of Swords

There's a medical condition — psychogenic aphonia — in which humans lose their voice because of fears, stress, and trauma. Though rare, it can also happen to someone who suppresses their opinions for too long and becomes afraid of ever "speaking their mind."

Just as the body only becomes strong through resistance, our minds are only sharpened by conflict, and arguments are the most common form of mental conflict. Certainly, arguments can be unpleasant, and some of us go far out of our way to avoid them. But suppressing what we really think for too long can weaken our minds, making us more easily controlled by others. And it can even cause physical harm to ourselves.

The Knight of Swords is the antidote to these fears of argument and other intellectual conflicts. When we are the Knight of Swords, we gallop bravely into such conflicts, courageously defending our beliefs and refusing to let others speak on our behalf. Especially in situations that seem to us as unjust or deceitful, the Knight of Swords won't hold his tongue.

Now, that hardly means we'll actually win these arguments. Sometimes we do, sometimes we don't. But what matters more is that we rushed to the challenge and fought for what we thought was right — whether we were actually right or not.

There is great power in this kind of approach to conflict, and the appearance of the Knight of Swords might be suggesting you consider it. Maybe there's something you really need to finally say to someone around you, or you've been spending more time trying to avoid a conflict than you ever would have spent actually facing it head on. Maybe the pressure of a situation or from others feels a lot like a knight charging at you, and it's time you ride out to meet this charge with your own sword drawn. But be clear: there's no guarantee you'll win in any such conflict. But it will sharpen your mind regardless.

As with all court cards, what is positive about this card can also be negative. The Knight of Swords doesn't wait until all the information is available before engaging a problem. If you tend to rush in without thinking very often, this card might instead be reflecting this back to you, and asking if it's time to take a more planned or less combative approach.

Queen of Swords

The champagne called Veuve Clicqot is named for the widow (*veuve*) of the man who founded the winery. While traditionally in French society it was the sons or brothers who would inherit a business after a man died, she instead took control of the small operation and turned it into the second best-selling champagne in the world.

The Queen of Swords is sometimes called the "widow" card, specifically because it refers to the kind of fierce independence often seen in women who've lost their husbands and thrived even more after those deaths. Yet you don't need to have lost a life partner to embrace that kind of self-sufficiency and independent spirit.

The Queen of Swords speaks to the deep confidence in our own abilities and insights that we reach many times in our lives. In such moments, we are able to rely on our experiences and accumulated knowledge to make important decisions, rather than expecting others to take the lead or allowing them to determine our fate. Especially for women, who are often socialized into deferring to the opinions of men, meditating on the power inherent in this card can be quite liberating.

If you don't currently have this kind of confidence in your life, the appearance of the Queen of Swords in a reading is probably encouraging you to embody it. You might already have all the information you need about a situation and just need to trust yourself more. Especially if you are single or experiencing a relationship change, you may greatly benefit from using this time to explore personal interests you might not otherwise have had time to pursue.

Some traditional interpretations also associate this card with editing. Here, the focus is on refining the way we communicate, choosing the best words for the best effects.

The fierce independence of the Queen of Swords can sometimes lead us to become disconnected from our body and emotional states, especially when we are engaged in intellectual pursuits. So, this card can sometimes also be a caution against isolating too much or living too much in your mind.

King of Swords

It's quite common to see interpretations of this card focus on its negative aspects, while only giving some mention of its positives. Perhaps that's because one of the strongest associations of the King of Swords is the kind of thought expressed in the philosophy of utilitarianism.

One of the main tenets of this philosophy is expressed in the idea of "the greatest good for the greatest number of people." Critics of this idea point out that it often leads to minority opinions — and those who hold them — getting ignored. That's particularly why interpretations of the King of Swords see it as a kind of strict, almost heartless intellectual approach to life.

There's certainly an impartiality here that can come across as pitiless, even cruel. Yet anyone who has ever needed to set a hard boundary with an abusive or reckless person has learned the deep power this card represents. Sometimes, we must sever relationships and cut out harmful influences, and the King of Swords can tell us how.

When you think of this card, think of a parent telling a child that he or she cannot play with matches. Sure, that child will feel like the parent is taking away something fun or is being heartless. But the parent knows something the child does not yet understand.

The King of Swords is like that parent, a kind of guardian presence or aspect of each of us. It's the part of us that sees things most rationally and can get us out of bad situations and also get us into good ones. In fact, that's exactly what our mind is best at. Though it cannot feel for us, or drive us onward, or manifest into the world, it can judge what is best and help us make decisions based on those judgments.

The King of Swords is the strongest and most refined use of our mind and intellect, which is why it's also often associated with judges, scientists, and any other profession that requires extensive mental training. But no matter your education, the intellectual sharpness of this card is also available to you, and we pass through this mode many, many times in life.

And as to the negatives, there is, of course, a real danger in relying too much on rational thought, and it is certainly possible to focus too much on the "greater good" instead of listening to less-heard voices. Each king cycles back to the page of the suit again, so remember the intellectual curiosity inherent in the Page of Swords if you are too long in this mode.

The Major Arcana

O, The Fool

Innocence, selflessness. A beginning, curiosity. A "leap of faith."
Letting yourself "not know."

The Fool is usually depicted as a young man, carrying a very small bag, walking merrily — and obliviously — towards a cliff. A dog follows him and appears to be trying to get his attention.

"Fool" is usually an insult, and "being foolish" is something no one wants to be. Yet, most of the really amazing and transformative things in life come when we do something foolish, unreasonable, and unsafe. Especially when we fall in love, we act in silly, embarrassing, and irrational ways.

Whenever we do something new, we become The Fool. We don't know what will happen, or how it will end. Not knowing can be scary, but it's also what makes things exciting. You can never be certain of anything in life — except death. All else is beautiful mystery.

When you see The Fool, consider how fear of the unknown can hold you back. Remember the curiosity you had as a child, how you didn't know how scary the world can be. Guess what? Even though things sometimes went very wrong, *you survived.*

The dog could be chasing him, or it could be warning him, or it could be a loyal companion coming along on the journey. Sometimes we are pushed into leaving our comfort zone. Sometimes, something or someone is trying to keep us there. And sometimes, friendship and love mean supporting someone when they take risks.

The cliff is the unknown, and always an important question when you see this card. What are you afraid of? What is the difference between being careless and carefree?

And the bag: it's small, huh? Turns out you don't really need much to be happy. You came into the world with no possessions, but have done very well anyway. Relax, and enjoy this journey.

I, The Magician

The recognition of our relationship to others.
Action, communication, manifestation, and play.

The Magician is usually shown holding a wand in one raised hand. He is often standing next to or behind a table filled with magical symbols, with the sign of infinity above his head.

Imagine what happens when you watch actors on a stage, or when, as a child, you played "make-believe." Something strange occurs: things that don't actually exist become real in those moments. It's as if there's another realm of meaning we forget about in normal life, but we can enter it — at least for a little while — when we play.

Play is an important idea to keep in mind when you see The Magician. In some of the oldest surviving Tarots, he was named *Le Bateleur*, which was an acrobat or carnival performer. Through their acting, they showed people wonders and what else might be possible.

Think on the double meaning of the verb, "act." What do the performers in a play do? Well, they *act*. But when we do something, we also *act*.

That's why this card is associated with communication, agency, imagination, and especially with manifestation. The Magician holds a wand towards the sky, but his other hand points firmly to the ground. An idea is just an idea until we ground it into reality. And the more we create, the more open we become to new ideas and to inspiration.

When you see The Magician, ask what you need to act upon, what you need to make real in the world. Nothing ever happens if we live only in our heads, and even the smallest actions change things. While The Fool seems to leave the future to chance, The Magician knows we have a say, too.

It's probably time you started something you've been putting off, and you need to begin somewhere. Don't be afraid of your influence or power. Don't worry that you don't know or aren't enough yet — you're only at the beginning, anyway. Go find out what else life can be, and do it with curiosity, playfulness, and wonder.

II, The High Priestess

Awareness of mystery, unconscious or hidden forces and influences.
Secrets, Stillness, Silence. Magic.

Often, the High Priestess (or *Papesse*) is shown sitting with an open book or a scroll in her lap. In many versions, she's between two pillars, sometimes with a crescent moon at her feet. Representations of The High Priestess vary very widely across various Tarot versions, and this is quite understandable. That's probably because, as with the dreamworld and unconscious forces she signifies, it's not easy to translate them into everyday symbolism.

We usually use the word "mystery" to define something we cannot explain or don't understand yet. In its oldest sense, though, the word referred to things that needed to be kept secret and required silence. In fact, the word "mute" comes from the same root as mystery.

The High Priestess is a card of mysteries, of silence, and of stillness, as well as the deep wisdom that comes from the body, rather than the mind. She tells us that it's okay to sit still, to not know the answer to a problem, and to wait out storms rather than trying to stop them.

Often when troubled, worried, or anxious, or when we are facing difficult decisions and situations, we try to think our way through things. Sometimes, we might also try to take actions that not only do not help, but actually make things worse. The agency and action taught by The Magician can only get us so far; sometimes the answers we need come when sit still, when we rest, and when we sleep.

When I see the High Priestess, I like to think of roots. They're the part of a plant we almost never see, and they do everything in darkness. Beneath the surface, beyond what we can see, is a whole world of secrets and mysteries giving life to what is visible.

It's okay to just let the still, silent, unseen forces in life work their magic, and to wait until we know the right course of action, the right decisions, or the right words to say. This is true even in the rare cases where The High Priestess might be pointing to the secrets of others. Again, we don't need to know everything, nor can we, and silence is sometimes the greatest kindness we can offer each other.

III, The Empress

Fertility, abundance, the creative force of earth and nature, birth.
Trust. The land and nature. Motherhood. The power of creation.

The Empress is a woman, often in royal clothing and holding a scepter in her hand, typically shown seated comfortably — sometimes even reclining — and surrounded by abundant nature. In popular depictions, there's often the alchemical sign for Venus, copper, and women (♀) shown on a heart-shaped shield. In some versions, she's pregnant.

Usually, you can breathe a deep sigh of relief when you find this card in a reading. The Empress is a card of fertility, of abundance, and of creation, and it's often telling you to relax, to enjoy the sensation of being alive and being a body, and to trust in the processes of life. Especially, it might be telling you not to rush or worry about the end results of something. As long as you're taking good care of what you already have, those you love, and especially of yourself, then all the other things will come in their time.

One key to understanding this meaning is to think about the way many ancient peoples believed women have an innate and deep connection to the land and the powers of growth and abundance. Deities of land, rivers, and agriculture were very often goddesses in these cultures, and humans needed to seek permission and consent from them in order to farm, hunt, fish, and otherwise live. In some cultures, kings were required to "marry" the land in order to gain the ability to rule, and the land could refuse. Even after an initial agreement, the land could later withdraw its consent due to the king's failure to treat it well, and those kings did not remain kings very long after that.

Besides being more environmentally sustainable, this way of thinking leads to the idea that human effort is not the only agency in creation, and we do not need to (and anyway cannot!) control those other forces. Think of a seed sprouting secretly beneath the soil, or a child growing hidden in its mother's womb. Though we can shape the conditions for life, in the end we must trust natural forces, the land, and life itself to do what they do best.

So, breathe a sigh of relief. Trust in life, trust the body that composes your existence, and try to live more fully so that there's room for even more life.

IV. The Emperor

Order, authority, structure, routine, and fatherhood.
The power of boundaries and the importance of protecting things.

Anyone who's ever tended a garden knows the uncomfortable moment of The Emperor. That's the moment when you look upon how much space you have, and then look at all the plants that are growing, and then realize you must decide which plants you'll let grow, and which ones you will not.

Just as The Empress represents abundance and growth, the Emperor represents boundaries, limits, and the difficult — but essential — choices we must make in order to sustain abundance. There is only so much time in our lives and only so much attention we can give. Without the power of The Emperor in our lives, we become drained, depleted, and unable to thrive.

The Emperor is the liberating power of the word "no." Saying "no" helps us set limits on things which take too much of our time and energy. It protects us from people who might abuse us, from bosses who demand too much from us, and from situations we don't want to be in. But saying "no" also helps us to say "yes" to the things which truly matter to us. Taking care of ourselves and those we love is only possible when we set limits on other activities. Saving money for important purchases is only possible when we limit how much we spend on unimportant things. And having strong and fulfilling relationships is only possible when we limit the time we devote to people who don't really matter to us.

The Emperor is also the importance of order, structure, and routine. Think about how much easier it is to cook in an organized kitchen, rather than a chaotic, messy one. Or how much easier it is to find your house key when you put it in the same place each time. Or how much safer it is to drive when everyone is obeying traffic laws. We need rules, just like a house needs structure or a garden needs borders. Sometimes those rules are arbitrary, and sometimes they are very unfair. But only in understanding why we need order can we learn to make better rules that help everyone thrive.

V. The Hierophant (or High Priest)

Tradition, religion. The importance of external expression of inner feelings. Education, guidance, and study. Love structured through formal commitment.

In some of the oldest tarots, the Hierophant is called the Pope, while in newer tarots, he's also called the High Priest. Regardless of what he's called, to anyone who has ever tried to reshape the "rules" of society — whether as an activist, a rebel, a freak, a punk, or even just a teenager — this card can seem like the enemy.

He shouldn't be seen that way, even though he does represent formal rules, tradition, structure, education, marriage, and a conservative adherence to prescribed formula. These are often aspects of society that seem outdated and sometimes even quite oppressive.

But if you try to bake a cake or bread for the first time, without a recipe and with no previous experience, you'll immediately see what The Hierophant is trying to teach you. "The way it's always been done" is sometimes actually the best way, we don't need to reinvent the wheel, and that seatbelt is in your car for a very, very good reason.

The word "Hierophant" comes from ancient Greek, and referred to a high priest's role in bringing people into sacred spaces. This points to another meaning of the card, which is that of guidance. Often, we need someone wiser and more experienced to teach us how to do something, to help us understand a situation, and especially to help us understand ourselves. Counselors, coaches, professors, mentors, elders, and teachers can all fulfill this role. So, too, can a formal religious or spiritual tradition.

Another important truth of this card is that external expressions help ground and manifest our internal feelings and beliefs. That's why it's often associated with marriage and other public rituals, each of which has a kind of magic of its own. Leaning on the strength of tradition can often liberate our passion in very powerful ways.

VI, The Lovers

The movement from control to surrender.
Death of the ego. Vulnerability and union. Desire.

There are a few cards for which the best advice is to stop, breathe, and look away from the Tarot for a moment, because they can provoke overwhelming emotions in us. One of those is Death, another is The Tower, a third is The Devil. The Lovers is the fourth.

Each of those cards points to a kind of death. In French, an orgasm is sometimes called *la petite mort*, "the little death," because we seem to lose consciousness at the moment of ecstasy. In intense love, it can feel as if we are dying a bit, losing ourselves, and forgetting all the things that were previously important to us. The self that we cultivated so well suddenly feels like a mere mask, and when it falls off we are completely naked before the Other.

Now, maybe The Lovers is referring to an actual love relationship — one you are in, one you want to be in, or one you were in. But it's also pointing to the destructive and creative power of love and desire, how it brings "little deaths" as it transforms the way we see the world and especially ourselves. Love changes us, and those changes have consequences over which we have little control.

The opposite of control is surrender, and surrender is a crucial idea of the The Lovers. Our ego is a kind of armor, protecting us from being vulnerable to others who might harm us. But to experience love and union, we must take off that armor, and that can be quite difficult to do. The Lovers is the moment we take that armor off, surrendering to someone we desire so much we're willing to risk getting hurt.

If the card isn't referring to an actual relationship, it's still pointing to this same process. There's a decision here, a choice between the safe and stable world of your self and the unpredictable world outside your bubble. Is there something or someone you desire? And if so, is that desire strong enough to upend your world?

VII, The Chariot

Mastery of opposing forces, integration. Victory or success through the development of our will and through self-knowledge. Also sometimes indicates actual journeys.

The first things you should notice about The Chariot are the two steeds pulling it forward. In many depictions, they are different colors, often one dark, one light. Then, notice the calmness of the charioteer, who appears to be driving without any significant effort.

Often, we can feel at war with ourselves, torn apart by competing desires and drives. Our desire for rest and solitude can sometimes seem like the enemy of our desire for friendship and activity. Or, our desire to feel safe can feel at war with our desire for excitement. We can then make the mistake of believing one of these drives is the "good" one, and the other is "evil."

The Chariot says otherwise. When these apparently opposite forces and drives within us are each given their place, we are able to accomplish incredible things. That's why one of the traditional meanings of this card is "victory." Learning to integrate both the creative and destructive aspects of yourself can take you very far in life.

The Chariot speaks to the success that comes through no longer fighting yourself. We often get in our own way, become indecisive, and cripple ourselves with doubt. That's because we are afraid of our will, of stepping into our power, and becoming who we are.

Look again at the charioteer's face. It's the same confident and calm look you see on the face of a musician or an athlete. They all make it look so easy, despite the years of hard work, practice, and discipline that went into getting to where they are now.

The Chariot might be telling you that you're at a similar place. Maybe you've worked for a long time to cultivate something, and the success you're about to have will make it all look really easy to everyone else. Maybe you just need to adopt that same calm confidence now, pick up the reins, and let those powerful aspects of yourself — and all the work you've done to understand them — guide you to where you want to go.

VIII, Strength

The mastery and confidence from The Chariot leads to self-assurance.
A light touch to life rather than force or violence.

Ever watched a tiny dog bark aggressively at a much larger, much stronger dog? Often, to the complete frustration of the smaller dog, the bigger one seems to ignore it completely.

That's what's happening in the Strength card, too. The woman gently holding an apparently fierce and vicious beast knows the same thing a large dog knows about smaller dogs. Most violence and aggression are only "sound and fury, signifying nothing," and true strength also involves knowing when you do not need to act. As is said in the *Tao Te Ching*,

> *The Master sees things as they are,*
> *without trying to control them.*
> *She lets them go their own way,*
> *and resides at the center of the circle.*

Keeping calm when others try to provoke you is quite easy when you understand your own power and what you are truly capable of. It's the same when life appears to throw challenges your way. Residing "at the center of the circle" — instead of getting caught up in the drama and chaos of the edges — doesn't mean avoiding life. Instead, it means maintaining a clear vision of which crises require you to act and which ones are just false alarms.

Many interpretations of this card see the woman as the master of the beast, but it's also worth seeing each of them as different aspects of ourselves. We are bodies, not just minds, and the artificial separation between these two aspects is at the root of many psychological and social problems in modern society. Embracing everything we are is also a source of strength, and body work like exercise, sport, dance, yoga, and martial arts can give you a deep confidence which feeds everything else in your life.

Find the center of the circle, and root there.

IX, The Hermit

Solitude and withdrawal to seek deeper wisdom, an "inner guide."
Understanding who we really are.

The Lovers, the Chariot, Strength, and now The Hermit are all trying to tell you something about the nature of the self, and each represents a kind of transformation of the ego. In The Lovers, we drop our armor to reach out to the world. In The Chariot, we learn to integrate our competing drives. In Strength, we learn our true power. And now, in The Hermit, we start to learn who we truly are.

Solitude can be a scary thing sometimes, especially since we rarely experience it. Even when we are alone, we often try to fill the silence with distractions like social media, movies, or music, anything to avoid truly being alone. But maybe we're not actually afraid of being alone at all, but rather afraid of spending our time with the one person —our self — who is always with us.

The Hermit tells us the same thing Irish priest John O'Donohue wrote in his book, *Anam Cara*: "the deepest things that you need are not elsewhere. They are here and now in that circle of your own soul." And only by withdrawing into silence can we actually find out what those things are, and also who we truly are.

Maybe it's time to take a break for a while. Go on a short trip by yourself (especially if other cards point to journeys) or at the very least turn off your phone and disconnect from the social world for a few days. Look at this the same way you'd look at a vacation with someone who really fascinates you, someone you'd like to get to know better. That someone is you.

More broadly, The Hermit is often hinting that you need some time to understand how you feel about a situation, or that you need some guidance or counseling. If you're feeling pressured by others, gently step away until you have more information, and create some space to just be with yourself.

X, Wheel of Fortune

Awareness of greater cycles and patterns. The wheel turns, and it must turn: knowing this helps us benefit from these cycles while not holding too tightly to being "on top."

Most interpret this card as a sign of good luck, especially if it's in a future position. On the other hand, showing up in a past position or upside down meant that the good times were about to end and hardship was coming.

That way of interpreting it might work for you, and you're welcome to use it. But I've long found this card makes much more sense when you see that it's not just pointing to fortune, but also to the turning wheel of life.

The world is full of cycles. The seasons are cycles, the moon's phases are cycles, and so are also the tides. Our lives, too, have cycles. Sometimes the wheel turns and everything feels easy, abundant, and beautiful. Then, the wheel seems to turn again and nothing seems to go right.

Becoming aware of these cycles can open up an entirely new realm of understanding in your life. Some moments are better for starting new things, other moments are better for building up what is already there, and some moments are best for enjoying the benefits of your work. The same is true in the social realm: sometimes you need to expand your circle, sometimes you need to deepen the relationships you already have, and sometimes you need to withdraw from some friendships which are no longer healthy.

When we try to work against these cycles, it can feel like nothing is working right. Or, when we benefit from good times but don't prepare for bad times, it can seem like the world is against us. There is actually a great danger in leaving things up to chance, or believing that the universe or some other external force is responsible for the good or the bad in your life.

On the other hand, understanding these cycles — and then learning to work with them instead of against them — can bring us the kind of "fortune" this card represents. So, in good times or in bad, try to understand what actions are best for those moments, and remember the wheel will turn again, and again, and again.

XI, Justice

Agency, our ability and responsibility to act in the world. An understanding of the effects of our actions and choices. An end to a feeling of victimhood or passivity.

Remember the core message of the previous card, the Wheel of Fortune. In it, we learn life has cycles and patterns. Justice, on the other hand, tells us we can also spin the wheel ourselves and create new cycles and patterns.

If I were to rename this card, I'd call it "Agency." Justice speaks directly to the power and responsibility each of us has in shaping our world. Though the decisions we make might be limited by the choices of others, we can never truly lose our agency unless we give it away.

Getting this card in a reading might not be the most pleasant experience, especially if you've been wondering why it feels like nothing is going right in your life. If so, Justice might be calling you to look at the role of your own actions in these difficulties.

Or, Justice could be referring to a hard choice you really need to make, or a difficult decision that you've been putting off. Here, it's helpful to remember the problem of "decision by indecision." That's when we put off making a choice for so long that this choice is no longer an option. For example, learning of a great job opportunity but then waiting too long to apply for it means we were actively choosing not to apply for it. Similarly, waiting too long to tell someone how we really feel about them means we were actively choosing not to tell them.

These are hard truths, and also very powerful ones. The blade of Justice can cut chains or end lives, and this card is reminding us that we hold that blade.

Remember the lessons of the previous cards. The Chariot and Strength both remind us that we have great power within us, The Hermit shows us we can find wisdom in the sanctuary of our soul, and the Wheel of Fortune tells us that we can know the best time to act. Now comes Justice, urging you to weigh the options with an unclouded mind, and then to act.

XII, The Hanged Man

This is The Fool again, calmly enduring or waiting. Usually an "initiation" of some sort, power forged from suffering, wisdom that comes when you no longer look for it.

In many Tarot decks, the person depicted in this card will probably look familiar. Yes, that's him — The Fool.

Throughout Europe, the time of Carnival was also called "the world upside down." Fools would be crowned king for a time, priests would marry donkeys, and all the usual rules of society were temporarily suspended.

The Hanged Man might be telling you that you're in such a time. Maybe your entire worldview has been shaken up, your beliefs and certainties all in upheaval. Perhaps everything you thought was true suddenly seems false, all the people and things you thought you knew no longer appear familiar.

There's nothing to do in such times but to wait, and that's what The Hanged Man is doing. In most depictions, he actually looks quite calm, even peaceful. After all, it's not a noose around his neck but rather a thin rope around his ankle. Also, one of his legs is crossed, as if he's just relaxing a bit. He doesn't actually seem to be in trouble at all.

We don't often like the word "surrender," especially because it's usually associated with the word "defeat." But there are plenty of times that surrendering is exactly what we want to do, like when we surrender to exhaustion and fatigue after a long day and then let ourselves go to sleep for the night. Passionate sex is also a kind of surrender, and so is just quieting ourselves in the face of overwhelming natural beauty.

The Hanged Man can sometimes refer to a moment of "social death." These are moments when others judge us — either rightly or wrongly — and nothing we do or say seems to be able to change their opinions. These are unavoidable moments in life.

If everything seems a bit crazy now, wait it out. Or, if it feels like everything is too difficult, get some rest. Especially if people are angry at you, or if it feels like you are being judged for your actions, the best thing to do might be to accept the moment and let it pass over you. Wisdom can come when we're not looking for it, and sometimes giving up a struggle can show us that we never needed to struggle in the first place.

XIII, Death

We die many, many times, and the physical death is just the last of these deaths. A death is coming or has happened. Time to compost what remains so there's room for more life.

Remember the advice I gave you when you see The Lovers in a reading? When you see Death, do the same thing: stop, breathe, and look away for a moment. And when you've done so, look again.

One of the most profound observations I've heard said about modern society is that we're obsessively terrified of death. We try to deny it at every turn, and we do everything in our power to postpone our demise. But as many indigenous elders have noted, this means we're never prepared for death when it actually happens.

A different way of understanding death is to see it as something that happens to us many times in life, not just at the end. When we learn something new, our previous ignorance has died. When a relationship ends, it can feel like a death. When we lose a job or a friendship, this is also a kind of death.

When you see death this way, you can come to realize that it's a deeply necessary part of life. In fact, *life is only possible because of death.* The food we eat — even if we're vegan — was once living and now no longer is.

If you have a compost pile in your garden, you already know the beautiful power of death. Dead wood, leaves, kitchen scraps, and other rotting things — all themselves corpses of once-living beings — can transform each other in the right combination into a substance so full of potential that even the most nutrient-hungry plants can explode into vibrant growth. From Death comes the grounds for new life.

This card is pointing to one of these moments. In a past position, it might be telling you to stop trying to hold on to something (a relationship, a conflict, an old habit or way of thinking) that is no longer present or useful to you. In a present position, there may be something that you need to stop denying and instead look at directly, or maybe you need to take what you need and compost the rest. And in a future position, especially if you're trying to get a sense of a possible outcome, an important change is on the horizon.

XIV, Temperance

The mixture of opposing aspects. Balance, flexibility, creation, patient effort.

Though usually associated with the idea of restraint and self-moderation, the word "temperance" originally referred to mixing things properly towards a desired effect. That's the ideal way to look at this card, not as a puritanical warning to abstain from something, but rather a reminder that you can consciously create balance in your life. And, from that balance, you can create even more powerful things.

Temperance could just as easily have been renamed the Alchemist or the Artist, since both these roles involve mixing things in balance to create something else. But keep in mind that creating balance doesn't necessarily mean putting everything in *equal* measure, but rather the *right* mixture.

How do you know what the right mixture is? The appearance of this card in a reading often suggests that you already do. That's why it's often seen as a very positive card, even in cases where it may also be telling you that you might be overdoing something.

To understand more about this right mixture, consider the sword in the Justice card. To forge an effective sword, the blade needs to be tempered to reduce the hardness of the steel. This makes the steel more flexible; without tempering, it would instead shatter when it struck something.

Notice that Temperance comes directly after Death? That's important. The first stage of alchemical transformation, *nigredo* — the destruction and decomposition phase — was essentially a kind of death. After *nigredo*, the substances were then separated into their opposing qualities and recombined in a new way.

Temperance is pointing to that moment of recombination. In a present position, it may be reminding you that everything you need is available, all the information is there, and all the competing feelings, opinions, and drives are waiting for you to weave them into a new tapestry. In a future position, it's likely telling you such a moment is coming.

If it's in a past position, though, give some thought to whether or not you've lost your sense of balance. Sometimes, we can find ourselves trying to go back to old habits and ways of thinking and therefore put off necessary transformations.

XV. The Devil

Getting in your own way. False limitations and beliefs. Something denied.

When you see The Devil in a reading, stop, look away for a moment, and then say "thank you," because he's there to tell you something really important and probably quite uncomfortable about yourself.

There are a lot of messy things in life. Things we don't like to admit, things we refuse to look at. We often think of ourselves as "good," as innocent victims, as moral actors in an immoral world. Then, when we cause harm, or are called to account for our actions, or when we are shown how the societies we live in are much more violent and unjust than we believe, we often get angry at the actual victims.

The Devil is everything we deny about ourselves. He's everything we try to pretend doesn't exist, everything we hide from others and from ourselves. He's the shadow, all the buried desires, fears, and other unpleasant things we push out of the light.

In most depictions of this card, The Devil looms over the man and woman from The Lovers card. They are bound by ropes or chains, but so loosely that they could very easily remove them. In fact, it's just as likely The Devil didn't actually imprison them — they probably did it themselves.

This is similar to the message in the Eight of Swords: problems are often of our own making, and we often don't really want to change anything. Like characters in a tragic comedy, we limit ourselves in almost hilarious ways, choosing the worst option time and again and then act shocked that we keep getting the same results.

Maybe you're getting in your own way again, or are about to. Maybe you're refusing to take responsibility for something, or lying to yourself about what your true motives really are. Maybe there's something you refuse to look at, and it's finally time you do. If you are caught up in a cycle of procrastination or addiction, you need to look at why you've gotten to this point, and what it is you are trying to avoid.

Especially, The Devil reminds us what happens when we ignore or suppress our feelings, desires, and fears. The longer we do so, rather than confronting them directly, the stronger and more destructive we make them.

XVI, The Tower

Destruction precedes creation. An external influence shaking up your world.
Something unpredictable, a sudden reversal of a situation.

In The Tower, lightning has struck a high structure, causing those atop it to plummet to the earth. In French, the words for "lightning strike" and "love at first sight" are the same, and this gives you a sense of the chaotic experience to which The Tower refers. In such moments, our world feels utterly upended by an encounter with someone or something outside ourselves, and we feel as if everything is about to change.

We often need external events or influences to shake up our world, especially when we've become too set in our ways. Of course, this can be quite scary, especially if we've become addicted to the sense of being in control or shutting out unpredictable things. When that happens, even the most minor inconvenience or unforeseen event can feel like a great crisis.

If that applies to you, consider the meaning of the word "crisis" in ancient Greek. Early doctors like Hippocrates used it to refer to the point in a disease where it became clear whether or not the person would survive or would die. In other words, the crisis point was a moment of revelation, not of emergency.

So, there's a sense of sudden enlightenment or illumination in The Tower. The situation has become suddenly very clear, the true nature of things is revealed, and what we thought was solid and sturdy crumbles around us. Like Death, this is something that occurs many times in our lives, and it is not a process to be feared.

The Tower can point both to difficult personal moments or powerful social shifts. In past positions, it might be telling you that the troubles you recently experienced were necessary moments of liberation, or reminding you not to put your trust in situations or people who have previously shown themselves untrustworthy, unreliable, or unsafe. In a present position, it may be reminding you that the chaos and confusion you are experiencing will make more sense once the dust clears. And in future positions, it might be advising you not to invest too much time or faith in a project that is unlikely to last.

XVII, The Star

Hope. Connection to the world, yourself, and sources of inspiration.

Usually, this card is a woman with one foot in a pool of water and the other on the ground, often pouring water from a pitcher back into the place from which it came.

The water in our bodies, the water vapor that forms clouds, the water buried deep in ice packs, and the water in every river and ocean in the world is all the same substance. When raindrops fall into a puddle, they become that puddle, and it would be useless to try to separate them again.

Similarly, it's said the iron in our blood was originally forged in distant stars. No matter how separate and isolated we might feel, we are each composed of the same elements as every other living thing on earth.

The Star directly follows The Tower for a very good reason, because it represents the core truths and meaning that persist beyond all our human structures. We are most ourselves and most alive when we feel connection, when all the barriers that separate people from each other and individuals from themselves no longer seem important.

The Star has strong resonances with the astrological sign Aquarius, the Water Bearer. It's a figure most associated with freedom of thought, universal humanity, and also creativity. There's also a sense in both Aquarius and The Star of drawing inspiration from deep wells, and then pouring out what is discovered back into the world for others to experience, too.

Just as electricity needs to be connected to both its source and its outlet to be useful, the currents of joy and meaning can only flow through us when we are likewise connected to both the sources of inspiration and outlets for its expression.

The Star is reminding you all this. This may be a moment you need to seek those deep wells, opportunities for expression, or both. If you've felt blocked or stagnant lately, this is a great moment to find new ways to connect to the world and to return to neglected sources of inspiration, peace, and joy.

XVIII, The Moon

Secrets, things hidden from view. Intuition, the wisdom of the body.

Traditionally, The Moon is associated with our unconscious, with dreams, with hidden knowledge, and especially with the mysterious source of knowledge that we call intuition.

The word "intuition" comes from the same word that became "tutor," and both originally referred to a helpful guardian that offered advice and watched over a person. Ancient and indigenous cultures — and even Christianity through the figure of the "guardian angel" — frequently understand intuition as an intimate spirit that gently guides a person, offering advice, warnings, and suggestions in a subtle way, very often through dreams.

Unfortunately, learning to listen to that guidance isn't a straightforward task. We often keep ourselves too busy to hear these soft whispers, and sometimes even actively ignore warnings that seem obvious in hindsight. People who overwork or spend much of their time on social media or in other distractions are particularly likely to become disconnected from the body. They then become confused when they get sick from stress or become injured through not exercising or stretching enough.

Also, when we are not skilled in interpreting these whispers, we can come to the wrong conclusions. Anxiety, for example, can lead us to feel like we are in danger or are being oppressed and insulted by others. However, that anxiety might just be a signal that we need more rest, or need to eat better, or to drink more water.

The Moon is telling you to give attention to these whispers, and also reminding you to interpret them in a cautious way. There's an endless wealth of knowledge in the body and in our dreams, but it cannot be easily translated into the realm of rational thought. Becoming friends with your intuition is a lifelong process, and you may need to cultivate new skills to learn how to do so.

XIX, The Sun

Joy and innocence. Optimism, with nothing hidden.

We often create false images of ourselves, masks we use to cover up the parts of us that we don't like and that we fear others will not like, either. Without opportunities to let these masks fall away, we can find ourselves defined by those fears and paralyzed by a sense there's something unloveable about us.

The Sun is the counterpart to The Moon. It's the clear illumination of the intellect, rather than the nuanced whispers of intuition. Truths are made brilliantly clear in its light, and we are naked before the world.

This card is very often seen as quite positive, and for good reason. Think on the way that everything feels much easier on a warm, sunny day, how the future seems bright and our problems feel less heavy. Everything seems possible on such days, as if joy and happiness are the default states of life rather than something we need to struggle to find.

Often, this card depicts a naked child on horseback surrounded by sunflowers. Sunflowers — along with an entire category of plants called heliotropes — appear to turn to face the sun as they grow, which is why in French they are called *tournesol* ("turn-suns"). What actually happens is that such plants grow more on parts facing the sun, and as the sun moves, the areas of growth change in response.

The Sun is urging you to lean into its light, and to let yourself grow in its warmth. There's a promise of success implied in its appearance — everything needed to become who we are is at hand. The key is in the innocence of the child, naked, unburdened by shame, fear, and self-doubt.

The appearance of this card in a present or any other position is probably telling you to connect to that childlike state and to enjoy the ease and vitality which creates the world. In a past position, it might also be suggesting that you look at a previous situation in a new light, as you may now have a better perspective and more information. And in a future position, things will soon be made clear and a new moment of growth and joy will come as certain as the day follows night.

XX, Judgement

A turning point. Significant decisions with powerful consequences. The need for self-reflection, an opportunity to change course for the better.

Usually, this card is illustrated with a scene of bodies rising from their graves, called forth by a trumpet blown by an angel. It's a scene evoking the Christian resurrection, an uncomfortable metaphor that has led many Tarot designers to change the card completely.

But Judgement isn't only a Christian idea, and it is not only at the end of life that we can look at the direction of our lives and the results of our actions. In fact, if we wait until the very end, we'll have missed countless opportunities, and we will die full of regrets. Judgement is telling you not to put off these crucial moments of self-reflection.

The previous three cards each refer to sources of knowledge. The Star is the inspiration that comes from connection, The Moon is the intuition of the body and our dreams, and The Sun is the warm light of reason. We need all three to be fully integrated and to see situations as they really are.

Judgement is what is made possible through that integration, as well as all the experience, wisdom, and self-development represented in each of the previous cards of the Major Arcana.

You may now be at a turning point in your life, with circumstances calling you — as with the angel's trumpet — to make a decision or a change that will determine what comes next. If this is the case, remember the lessons of The Star, The Moon, and The Sun, and if the possible consequences of your decision seem potentially world-ending, look at the name of the card that follows this one, and laugh.

In fact, there's a lot of healing represented in this card, especially if you've been haunted by earlier trauma or have had a difficult time forgiving others or yourself. In any position in a reading, Judgement might be pointing to this healing.

Judgement is an especially great card to see if you are trying to kick an old habit or to get out of a self-destructive cycle, because it suggests that your conscious efforts will have profound effects.

XXI, The World

Completion, fulfillment, unity.

When I see this card, I always think of the following lines from a T.S.
Eliot poem:

"At the still point of the turning world. Neither flesh nor fleshless;
Neither from nor towards; at the still point, there the dance is...
..Except for the point, the still point,
There would be no dance, and there is only the dance."

In some of the oldest Tarots, the figure in this card has both masculine
and feminine features, evoking the union and integration of opposing
forces. In most versions, the figure is inside an oval wreathe with one leg
crossed as in The Hanged Man.

The World was always where The Fool was heading, though he didn't
know how he'd get there. In fact, had he known, he might never have
started the journey in the first place. And he had plenty of opportunities to
turn back.

The World represents the completion of a cycle, the arrival at a
destination, the end of a long process of understanding. A moment of
fulfillment has arrived, something has been achieved, and the long work to
get to this point suddenly looks like it had been very easy all along.

But as with Death and Judgement, or with the tens in the Minor Arcana,
it doesn't mean a final end. We will be The Fool many times in our lives,
and will become the dancer in The World many times as well.

Still, this card's appearance very likely means you can celebrate,
especially if it appears in a present position. You can let yourself enjoy the
results of your hard work, bask in the praise you receive from others, and
dance in this moment of completion. If it's in a past position, it might also
be telling you the same thing. Maybe you didn't even notice that you had
completed a difficult time and that you can now relax. Or, that the current
situation is the result of such a completion, and you might want to
contemplate how they are related.

In a future position, you can look forward to such a moment soon, though
there may still be some conflict within you waiting to be resolved. If so,
look at that conflict not as a war, but as a dance.

Card Index:

About The Author

Rhyd Wildermuth is a druid and writer. Originally from the foothills of Appalachia, he now lives in the foothills of the Ardennes.

He's the author of eight (well, now nine) books, including *Being Pagan: A Guide to Re-enchant Your Life* (also from RITONA) and *Here Be Monsters: How to Fight Capitalism Instead of Each Other* (from Repeater Books).

He's been reading Tarot for himself — and occasionally for others — for at least twenty-seven years, and he spends his free time equally between the forests, his garden, and the gym. He writes at Rhyd.substack.com.

About RITONA

Named for the Celtic goddess of river-crossings, RITONA is an esoteric, occult, and political publisher devoted to a more tolerant world through pluralism. By pluralism, we mean a deep acknowledgment that others have different worlds and different centers of meaning. Only by acknowledging these differences as deeply human can we then find true commonalities across cultures, religions, and political frameworks.

We also advocate for respect for indigenous and non-industrial ways of being in the world. Simpler, less destructive, and more place-based relationships between humans and the rest of the world have been the primary kinds of relationships for most of human history. The "benefits" of industrial civilization can never outweigh the great harm done to humans and the rest of the world. Find more about our books, our courses, and read our online journal at: ABEAUTIFULRESISTANCE.COM.

www.ingramcontent.com/pod-product-compliance
Lightning Source LLC
Chambersburg PA
CBHW020527160726
47992CB00005BA/2287